Doris
Herman's
Preschool Primer
for Parents

Doris

Herman's
Preschool Primer
for Parents

A Question-and-Answer Guide to
Your Child's First School Experience

Doris Herman

A LIVING PLANET BOOK
JEREMY P. TARCHER/PUTNAM
a member of Penguin Putnam Inc.
New York

Most Tarcher/Putnam books are available at special quantity discounts for bulk purchases for sales promotions, premiums, fund-raising, and educational needs. Special books or book excerpts also can be created to fit specific needs. For details, write Putnam Special Markets, 375 Hudson Street, New York, NY 10014.

Jeremy P. Tarcher/Putnam
a member of
Penguin Putnam Inc.
375 Hudson Street
New York, NY 10014
www.penguinputnam.com

Library of Congress Cataloging-in-Publication Data

Herman, Doris.
    Doris Herman's preschool primer for parents : a question-and-answer
guide to your child's first school experience / by Doris Herman.—
1st trade pbk. ed.
        p.   cm.
    ISBN 0-87477-938-3
    1. Education, Preschool—Parent participation—United States.
2. Education, Preschool—United States—Miscellanea.   I. Title.
LB1140.35.P37H47   1998   98-4007 CIP
372.21—dc21

Printed in the United States of America
10   9   8   7   6   5   4   3   2   1

Book design by Mauna Eichner

Acknowledgments

Thanks, love, and appreciation go first and foremost to my husband Don, and to my children, Joe and his wife Liz, Brenda and her husband Michael, and Josh and his wife Andy, for their unfailing humor and support, and for their expert advice and encouragement.

Very special thanks go to Shelley Remer, the extraordinary director of my school, Gan HaYeled at Adas Israel Synagogue, for her guidance and expertise. Also to Judith Mars Kupchin, Charlotte Muchnick, Veneeta Acson, Louie Dweck, Linda Robinson Walker, Susie Blattner, Leona Chase, Rose and Louie Segal, and to all of my Puppy Room parents who asked those important questions.

I am particularly indebted to Joshua Horwitz and Julie Kuzneski at Living Planet Books for their bright ideas and sound advice along the way. Finally, heartfelt thanks to my talented editor, Mitch Horowitz, who saw the message in my manuscript and made it into a book.

This book is dedicated to three very special preschoolers,

my grandchildren Ricki, Jennifer, and Benjamin (Jamie).

I wish them beautiful beginnings and

joyful memories of preschool.

And to the parents of the hundreds of children

who walked through my classroom door and into my arms.

Contents

Transition to Preschool: Your Child's—and Your—First Days

What You and Your Child's Teacher Should Know About Each Other

8. Transportation and School Attendance 111

9. "What If My Child . . . ?" 119

Foreword

By Rory Zuckerman, host, Rory's Place, *on*
The Learning Channel, and national spokesperson for Head Start

When it comes to parenting, we're all beginners. The learning curve starts the day you bring your first child home from the hospital and continues for a lifetime. Looking back at my own experience raising two sons, I can remember nothing more nerve-racking than selecting the right preschool and sending my son off that first day.

After two years of barely letting him out of my sight, how was I supposed to trust a stranger to love him and watch over him as I did? How much time away from home could he handle? Two days a week? Three? Five? Half or full days?

What program and curriculum did he need? Should he be learning to count and read already, or just learning to play with other kids? Should I send him to a Montessori preschool, or the one run by the local temple?

Facing these seemingly unanswerable questions made me want to holler, "Mom!"

The problem was that my mom didn't know any more about preschool than I did. When I was growing up, preschool didn't exist. There were nursery school programs of various stripes, but it's only been in the past twenty years that we've come to realize just how crucial those first years are for children's learning and development. Now we know that during ages two to five, children's brains are growing at their fastest rate, and it's when they're learning their most formative lessons about themselves and the world around them.

As the national spokesperson for Head Start and the host of a children's educational TV show, *Rory's Place*, I've come to understand just how critical these years are to a child's success in grade school and beyond. But if you go to a bookstore, you'll be hard-pressed to find any useful guidance about choosing between day care and preschool, or among the many kinds of preschool programs available. And you certainly won't find books that address your everyday questions about your child's first educational experience: What are the safety issues I should be concerned about? How should I prepare my child for the transition into a strange classroom? What if he cries? What if he bites?

So it was with great trepidation that I took my son's hand and walked him to his first day of class. Imagine my relief when I found a warm and wise woman waiting for my son and me. Her name was Doris—or Teacher Doris, as my son and his classmates called her. I quickly came to think of her as my friend, confidante, and surrogate mother, as did every other parent in her Puppy Room. Only years later did I come to appreciate the great gift that she had bestowed on my son: a positive first experience of school and of his teacher—an experience that has stayed with him all his life.

I can only describe Doris as a natural—intuitive and graceful in her relationships with children. But her seeming ease masks a deliberate agenda and high expectations of her young charges. She promotes friendship through community. She provides play experiences that illustrate life experi-

ences. She models values that her students carry with them into adulthood. Most impressive is how she takes an impromptu experience and turns it into a teachable moment.

When children are frustrated or afraid or confused, they look for our reaction. Most of us identify with their anxieties. They then pick up on our feelings, and the cycle only intensifies, usually ending in tears or tantrums and lost tempers on both sides. What Doris sees is a teachable moment—a chance to steer a child toward understanding and away from fear, or toward growth and sharing and away from selfishness. But most of all, her technique is about turning a child toward his or her essential self—without fear or shame, with pride and excitement.

This critical skill of finding teachable moments and using them wisely is one that both teachers and parents need to learn. This is when real education happens. Listening to Doris helps us develop our own sense of timing and our own ideas about what we want our children to know.

Doris is a master at involving parents as partners in their child's learning. Watching her is the best education for parents. How does she develop the sense of wonder and discovery? How does she consistently communicate unconditional love for each child? How do we learn when to love our children up close and when to love them from a distance?

We can't all have the experience of observing Doris's classroom in person, and not every mother is lucky enough to have a Teacher Doris to entrust her child to. But this book offers us an exciting opportunity of a different sort. Here is a collection of Doris's wisdom, insight, and knowledge, arranged according to a table of contents that is the answer to every

parent's prayer! When I scan Doris's Q&A contents, it's as if she had been reading my mind. And it's no accident. Doris has based this book on the most frequently asked questions she's heard from parents over the decades and the need-to-know answers she's provided. It's a resource that will be treasured by parents and teachers of preschoolers alike.

But this is much more than a question-and-answer book. Lodged within the text is a personal teaching philosophy that all parents can take home with them. It's a lesson of respect for our children—as they are. The toughest thing about being a good parent is to encourage a child's authentic self to emerge and blossom unfettered by our preconceived wishes and expectations. Doris has a way of using love to bring out the best that is in every child. It's a gift that few people possess, but we can all learn by her example.

What's her secret? It sounds simplistic, but it's all about love. Attentive love that holds up a mirror to a child's best self and reveals a world of imagination and discovery that is the widest field any child can play in. Love is the key that unlocks the door of exploration and flings it open wide.

And once that happens, no one can ever slam it shut.

So welcome to this wonderful book, and the new world that's opening for your child. Read it once for information—about programs and health regulations and class sizes and admissions policies. Then read it again—for lessons in unleashing your children's minds and hearts, and letting go of your fears about releasing them into their own wide world.

Introduction

Why I Wrote This Book

For twenty-five years, an endless stream of wonderful children have walked through my classroom door and into my arms. In their wake are the parents, brimming with worries and questions.

The goal of my classroom is to ensure that my students' first school experience will be a journey filled with learning, trust, affection, and growth. More difficult for me and for every other teacher of very young children is convincing parents to trust us with their most precious possessions. I spend a great deal of time holding parents' hands, calming their minds, and answering questions. "What if my child isn't happy?" "What if she gets sick?" "What if he doesn't get along with the other kids?" "What if . . . What if . . . What if . . . ?" I have answered these questions for twenty-five years, and each and every question was important.

When my own children began having children, they asked me these same questions. I was amazed to discover that there were no authoritative books addressing the anxieties that plague parents of children entering preschool. Encouraged by my own children and the parents in my school, I wrote this *Preschool Primer for Parents* to help dispel the mystery and misconceptions about what takes place during a typical preschool day. Parents are sometimes reluctant to bother a teacher with a seemingly frivolous question, but no concern about a child is ever frivolous. Parents need a book they can turn to in the middle of the morning or the middle of the night—whenever a question about their young child nags at their heart.

In my experience, helping children separate from parents in the first year of school is far easier than helping parents separate from children. While parents are excited about the beginning of their child's educational journey, they are also anxious, realizing that preschool is the important first step in a process that will shape their child's growing and developing mind. Twenty years ago, preschool was simply nursery school, a day-care setting where children could play while their parents worked. It's only recently that we've come to understand just how critical the preschool years are to the development of a child's social, cognitive, language, and motor skills. A positive preschool experience can set a joyful pattern for a lifetime of learning; a bad experience can do just the opposite.

In this book I've given examples of what happens in my particular school. Each school does things differently and has its own style and strengths. As you read this book and go through the process of assessing preschools, keep in mind that no school has everything. As parents you need to distinguish between what you need to have versus what is nice to have for your child. Some parents believe a well-equipped playground is the most important for their active youngster; others may look for whichever school is most affordable and closest to their home. Keep in mind, however, that the *safety and well-being of your child should be top priority.* Never compromise on the issue of safety. If a school is lacking in other areas, it does not mean that it is not a good school. If you feel that you have found a school that is safe and a good match for your child but is lacking in some areas that could be improved or changed, you can advocate for those changes by joining the PTA or talking with the director.

This *Preschool Primer for Parents* is not a book about child development theories, educational philosophy, or psychology. There are many books devoted to those topics. This book, like my classroom, is centered on the experiences of children. It's an easy-to-read guide that anticipates parental concerns and tries to address them with insight, compassion, and humor. I've tried to make it a hands-on and practical primer that will educate and empower parents. The question-and-answer format is modeled after the ongoing dialogue I have with the parents of my preschoolers, covering a wide range of topics, from toilet training to safety to separation anxiety.

For every child I have hugged, I have held a parent's hand. I hope this book will be the warm outstretched hand every first-time parent is looking for.

Considering Preschool
for Your Child

What are preschool, nursery school, and day care?

There are a variety of terms to describe a child's first school experience. Years ago, pre-kindergarten school experiences were called *nursery schools*. That term is still used today and is generally interchangeable with *preschool*. Because kindergarten is thought of as "real school," any school that comes before is preschool. So in this book I use the term *preschool*. These educational programs for very young children have proved to be invaluable, because of what we now know about the importance of the development of a child's social, cognitive, language, and motor skills in the early years.

Preschools are schools that provide programs for children who are younger than kindergarten age, typically between the ages of two and five. These programs provide quality care, socialization, enrichment, play, and education. Opportunities for learning are available in these group settings that are difficult to duplicate at home. Children who attend preschools have the advantage of being able to interact with groups of children of similar ages, while taking part in professionally planned activities and rich experiences that will provide the basis for later learning. All this in a safe and regulated environment.

Licensed preschools offer half-day programs, usually three to four hours, for children between the ages of two and five. Some schools include parent and toddler programs for younger children as well. Many schools also offer extended-day options, where children may be dropped off before official school hours, stay for an afternoon program until around 3 P.M., and/or stay later for after care. Classes are held from September to June, with some schools offering camp-type programs in the summer and sometimes regular summer-school programs.

Day care encompasses a wider range of programs that may include preschool. Generally speaking, day care offers day-long and year-round programs to conform to the schedules of working parents, unlike preschool schedules, which may be limited to a half day, have summer breaks, and follow the public school holiday schedule.

Day care and preschool should offer comparable educational and social experiences, and many day-care centers now prefer to be called all-day preschools. All day-care centers must conform to local and national standards and regulations. The National Association for the Education of Young Children (NAEYC) offers the opportunity for accreditation to both preschools and day-care centers. Both should offer equal opportunities for social and cognitive learning.

Basically, a quality learning environment for young children can be found in either. Enforcement of regulations may vary from state to state, however, so it is vital for parents to investigate thoroughly any center or school they may be considering. The best way to research the strengths and weaknesses of a potential program is by visiting the facility and sitting in on actual sessions.

What do children do in preschool?

If you ask young children what they do in preschool, they will probably answer, "Play." They are playing. But within the realm of play, they are doing much, much more.

Play is the way children learn about themselves and their world. They need to investigate, discover, touch, smell, and pretend. In a group, they learn to share, make choices, resolve conflicts, negotiate, and communicate effectively. Children learn to feel capable and good about themselves through play. The opportunity to learn all these wonderful skills is available through play with other children in preschool.

Specifically, a typical morning or afternoon in school will provide:

★ An activity period—free play

★ Singing and music

★ Art experiences

★ Movement

★ Reading and books

★ A snack

★ Circle or meeting time

★ Outdoor play

There will be time for group play as well as the opportunity for solitary play. Structured group activities and unstructured playtime are also important parts of a program. In addition, most schools offer special events, such as puppet shows, concerts, and field trips.

Schools may vary in scheduling, but every quality program will provide for the intellectual, emotional, physical, and social needs of young children through play.

Does my child have to go?

No. No child has to go to preschool. Preschools are there for enrichment. Children who attend have the advantage of learning to function as part of a group, learning routine, and acquiring social skills. Children entering kindergarten without having attended preschool will certainly learn all these things anyway. Whether or not to send your child to preschool should be a personal choice.

Some of the acknowledged advantages of preschool are:

★ To expose children to a variety of experiences for imaginative play with other children

★ To promote a sense of independence and self-esteem

★ To enable children to learn to function as part of a group

★ To learn to share and take turns

★ To stimulate children's natural curiosity

★ To facilitate proficient speech and language

★ To explore a wide variety of arts-and-crafts materials

★ To be exposed to a variety of age-appropriate books and literature

★ To learn about the environment and the world around them

★ To be exposed to mathematical concepts

★ To promote physical strength, coordination, and stamina

★ To learn about music through songs and instruments

★ To promote a love of learning

Some parents prefer to keep their two- or three-year-old children home with them. Many mothers who do not work outside the home enjoy having their little ones with them full-time and plan activities to do together, such as baking cookies, going to the zoo, or working in the garden. If this arrangement is comfortable and satisfying for parents and children, wonderful.

Enrolling your child in preschool, however, should not preclude you from enjoying these activities on nonschool days. Most preschools offer two or three morning options for young children, which allow plenty of time for parent-and-child togetherness.

How do I know whether my child is ready?

There are questions you should ask yourself in order to determine whether your child is indeed ready for the experience of preschool. Your child's readiness may be determined by evaluating her physical endurance, her napping needs, her overall health and stamina, and whether or not she is ready to separate. Is she able to express her needs either verbally or nonverbally? If she seems physically and emotionally ready, you may then ask yourself:

★ Is your two- or three-year-old bored at home?

★ Do you feel pressured to plan activities for your child every day?

★ Does your child enjoy being with other children?

★ Are you constantly looking for play dates for your child?

★ Is your child willing to be away from you for short periods of time?

If you answered yes to most of these questions, your child may well be ready for preschool.

How much will preschool cost?

The cost of preschool programs varies dramatically. Geographic region and hours of attendance tend to be the major factors in how much it costs to send a child to preschool, but type of program and quality also count. A high-quality program should be your top priority, but bear in mind that the highest-quality schools are not necessarily the most expensive. For example, one school director I spoke to in the South explained that some very reputable church-affiliated programs in his area charge as little as $125 per month for an all-day program.

To illustrate these regional variations, I telephoned one school from each of the urban and suburban areas listed below to find out what it charged per month in 1998. Rural schools in these regions would probably cost considerably less.

Region	Less than half day	Half day	Full day
Grosse Pointe, Michigan	$445	$675	$975
New York City		500	900
San Mateo, California	280	320	460
Altoona, Pennsylvania		210	300
Mobile, Alabama	225	305	395

The U.S. Census Bureau has figures that provide a very rough basis of comparison. I say rough because those figures are for 1993, do not apply specifically to preschool but to all forms of child care (preschools, family day care, and in-home babysitting), and are not adjusted for variations in hours spent in child care. The Census Bureau found that child care costs an average of $370 per month in the Northeast and $305 per month in the Midwest and the South. Child care in metropolitan areas was more expensive—an average of $345 per month—than in rural areas.

As you do research to find a preschool that is right for your child, cost may very well be a determining factor in your decision and should be one of the first questions you ask the director of each school. Learning the costs of several schools in your area will give you a basis for comparison shopping. Also bear in mind that many preschools have scholarships and financial-aid packages. If the school you're interested in costs significantly more or less than other schools, ask the director for the reasons behind this discrepancy.

When should I register my child?

For most preschools, the number of openings in various classes changes from year to year. Some schools have many openings each September for two- and three-year-olds, and others have very few. The following year, the number of openings in the same school may change. Some schools are flexible about age requirements, and others ask that the children be two years old by September. There are also schools that begin new two-year-old classes several times a year—for example, September and January—or have a rolling admission policy in which children may be admitted anytime during the school year if there is an opening.

If you live in a part of the country where schools are actively searching for preschool-age children to fill vacancies, you can probably relax about registration. But if you live in an area where admissions and school vacancies are at a premium, the earlier you begin the process, the better. If you want your child to be enrolled in a specific preschool at the age of two, you should obtain information about enrollment a year in advance. You will not be making a commitment; you are just gathering information.

Dates for submitting applications vary from one part of the country to another. Ask the school to be specific about registration dates. When you call for information a year ahead, ask about other admissions policies:

★ Is it first come, first served?

★ Is registration determined by age?

★ How many openings will be available the following September for children your child's age?

★ When is the latest you can register and be assured a spot for your child?

Most schools charge a nonrefundable application fee to apply. For those who are sure that they have found the right

school and are actually enrolling their child, there is usually a heftier nonrefundable registration deposit. For those applying to more than one school, expect to pay those nonrefundable application fees and hope your child is accepted to the school you really want.

Finding the
Right Preschool for
Your Child

How do I begin looking for a school?

Your priority will be to find a preschool that offers a high-quality program, is affordable to you, and is geographically convenient. It may take time and effort to research and locate a good school for your child, or it may be as simple a task as asking friends and acquaintances whose children are having positive experiences in school.

Ask your local librarian to show you the library's list of resource books for finding schools in your area. You can also contact the National Association for the Education of Young Children (see Appendix, p. 155). This association provides comprehensive information about child-care options throughout the country.

Other good sources of information are your child's pediatrician, your local church or synagogue, public schools, or other local organizations. When you have compiled a list of acceptable choices, it's time to visit the schools. (See question 12.)

Are licensing and accreditation important?

Absolutely. The primary purpose of licensing is to ensure the health and safety of the children enrolled in a day-care or private preschool facility. Every school should be licensed by

the governing body of its state or local agency. If a school is not licensed, it means that the facility or school does not meet established requirements for health and safety. Look elsewhere.

In addition, there are a growing number of preschools in the United States that have been accredited by the National Academy of Early Childhood Programs, a division of the National Association for the Education of Young Children (NAEYC). This means that the school has undergone an extensive and comprehensive internal evaluation of every single aspect of its staff and early childhood program. It has met the stringent requirements for eligibility, has fulfilled all the criteria for high-quality early childhood programs, and has been judged by a commission to be worthy of accreditation. Programs that are accredited have achieved professional and public recognition as providers of high-quality care and education of young children. These schools have met standards much beyond what is expected by state and local governing agencies.

This does not mean that schools not accredited by the NAEYC are not good schools. A school may be newly established or may be working toward accreditation.

Academics or play—which type of program is best for my child?

Preschool Methods

TRADITIONAL PLAY-BASED AND ACADEMIC PRESCHOOLS

★ Lots of time is provided for free play, along with varying amounts of academics presented at an age-appropriate level.

★ Children are grouped by age.

★ Emphasis is placed on cognitive development, with specific expectations and educational goals.

★ Music, art, and creative movement are a part of most programs, along with a mix of free choice and structure.

MONTESSORI SCHOOLS

★ Life skills and academics are taught during daily "work" with special sensory learning materials in the classroom.

★ Emphasis in a Montessori school is on self-directed learning with preschool children from ages two and a half to five or six years in one preschool classroom.

★ Children are encouraged to work at their own pace.

★ The same teacher usually remains with the children in the early years.

WALDORF SCHOOLS

★ Emphasis is on creativity in all areas of a child's schooling.

★ Importance of creative play is linked with creative thinking and healthy development.

★ Focus is away from academics and toward allowing the young children the time, freedom, and space to develop to their own capacity.

★ Much hands-on learning with paint, craft materials, music, drama, and dance.

Many preschools offer academically based programs, which is to say, programs that present reading and math preparation along with play and social development. Computer education has even been added to some preschool curriculums. Many parents feel that it is important to give their children a head start in academics. The challenge for preschools with academic programs is to keep the learning fun and developmentally appropriate to each age group, while also stressing the importance of play.

Play-based programs encourage children to learn through play. Some structured learning is incorporated into the daily program, but the emphasis is on divergent thinking and discovery through free play. For instance, children learn the concepts of math and science by manipulating clay, sand, and water. By measuring, pouring, weighing, and molding, they discover these concepts for themselves. Children enjoy these open-ended activities because there are no right or wrong judgments. Playing with building blocks offers opportunities for problem solving, math-skill building, communication-skill building, and sharing. Children who are allowed to experiment with these materials develop creative and divergent thinking, as well as gross and fine motor skills needed later for coloring, drawing, and writing. While children play, they use language to express themselves by communicating thoughts, feelings, and ideas. Many studies support the theory that a substantial amount of self-initiated play is essential to future academic learning. These studies have shown, in kindergartners and first-graders, a correlation between proficiency in sociodramatic play and achievement in reading comprehension and writing. My personal feeling is that children will have the rest of their lives to read and write, but they have only those precious first sixty months to play.

It is important for parents to assess their *own* educational philosophy and to understand both types of preschool programs before making a choice. The best way to do this is by visiting and observing a class in each school under consideration. A play-based school should incorporate some structure into the daily program, such as circle time and group learning activities, rather than whole mornings of free play, which some feel is akin to supervised babysitting. In a more academic preschool, no matter how much parents want their child to have a head start in learning numbers, counting, and letters, if academics seem to be pushed onto the children, that school is not a good choice. Choose instead an academic preschool that incorporates academics into play and games without pressuring or drilling the children.

Other types of schools are perhaps less traditional in their approach to preschool education but share the goal of educating children while enhancing self-esteem and instilling a love of learning. One such system is the Montessori schools. In Montessori schools, learning occurs through an educational process, rather than the play-based philosophy of the traditional preschool. Instead of toys, a Montessori school is rich in concrete learning materials to teach letters, numbers, abstract ideas, and life skills that are intended to preserve the integrity of the individual child whatever the age. There is multi-age grouping of children rather than the traditional grouping by age. The theory is that the younger children will model learning and behaviors from the older children, and assisting the younger children reinforces learning for the older children. Children do not change classes and teachers each year but remain with the same group. Order is important in the Montessori classroom, and children are taught to organize and care for their classroom as a part of their life-skills education.

Another method-based program is the Waldorf, or Rudolf Steiner, school program. The philosophy of the Waldorf schools is that modern children are hurried in the field of cognitive development, so the emphasis is on play and creativity. The children in these schools learn by physical and hands-on experiences in the arts, rather than through academics.

The progressive schools are identified with John Dewey and have the explicit philosophy that children learn through play. Play is seen as the children's work, and these schools focus on free play even more than the traditional play-based schools. Children work together in groups with materials that encourage process rather than project results. Progressive schools are often referred to as total-child or whole-child schools.

Every private school has a distinct character, style, and educational philosophy. Most preschools fall somewhere between the all-play or all-academic philosophies. The majority of parents are most comfortable knowing their children are getting a balance of free play and healthy structure while learning. Traditional schools have adopted many of the styles and philosophies of method-based schools and present a balanced curriculum.

Community parent-cooperative schools offer two advantages over other kinds of preschools: lower cost and greater involvement in your child's preschool experience. Generally, these schools have a play-based curriculum. In most cooperative preschools, there is a certified teacher in each class, with parents taking turns serving as support staff in the school, as either classroom assistants or administrative assistants. These preschools are less expensive because parents volunteer on a rotating basis, so school overhead costs are not as much as in preschools that have large salaried staffs. Parents should expect the same standard of excellence in a cooperative school as in any other. In addition, parents will need to know what is expected of them so they can evaluate whether or not they can make the time commitment to the school.

No matter what type of preschool you are considering, do your research by sending for brochures and learning as much as possible about the many types of programs and the different types of preschools. This research should be done before scheduling visits to the schools under consideration.

I teach at a play-based school and take every opportunity to inform the parents that along with play, pre-academics are indeed incorporated into the daily program. When parents come into the classroom to observe, I explain that cleanup time is a very important part of our day. I invite the parents to watch as the children gather the cars and trucks to put in the vehicle basket. The scattered crayons go in the crayon box, the markers in the marker box, the dolls in the cradle, the dishes and play food on a shelf in the kitchen cabinet, and the scattered puzzles and manipulative toys in their own containers. Parents are impressed with the enthusiasm with which little hands are "cleaning," but they are far more impressed when I point out that what they have just witnessed are pre-math skills in progress. The children have accomplished sorting and categorizing. It's math!

What about religion-based schools?

Many churches and synagogues house preschools in the same buildings. These schools may incorporate religious observances and practices within the framework of the daily preschool program, which can be very enriching for the children. Prayers may be recited, religious holidays and festivals celebrated, religious songs sung, and specific religious tenets taught—all on an age-appropriate level. While the warmth of religious traditions is enjoyed and celebrated by all the children attending, the population of these types of preschools may lack diversity.

When parents of different religions enroll their children in a religion-based preschool, one might expect problems. Actually, the opposite is usually true. If parents have resolved intermarriage issues relating to child rearing, the decision to enroll the child in a religion-based preschool can be made with the consent and agreement of both parents. The child learns the religion and customs of the school attended and may participate in celebrating the holidays of the other parent's religion at the grandparents' home. It is workable when the parents agree to make it work.

Occasionally, parents choose to send their children to a preschool based on a religion other than their own because of its first-rate program. Since religion-based schools usually don't modify their programs for children of other religions, parents need to explain to their children that they will be learning about the holidays and religions observances of that particular school even though their family practices a different religion.

What if my child has special needs?

Many private preschools have expanded their programs to include children with special needs (refer also to question 25). These include children with hearing and/or visual impairments, learning disabilities, chronic illnesses, minor birth defects, and any conditions that impair function. These children can enjoy all of the benefits of preschool before going on to public school. The parents of a child with special needs will have to do extra research to find a preschool that will meet the physical, educational, and emotional needs of their child.

If your child has special needs, you certainly need to arrange for a conference with the director of each of the schools you are considering before deciding on a school. If the school you have chosen has accepted your child, you may be assured that much thought and care has gone into the decision and that the staff involved has made a commitment to provide a secure and nurturing environment.

It is necessary for the school to have as much information as possible about your child. It might be wise to arrange for a conference with your child's therapists or service providers, the school director, and the teaching staff so that everyone involved knows, understands, and is in agreement

with the expectations and goals for your child. Discuss how much information you would like the other parents in your child's class to have and how and by whom it should be presented. If necessary, arrangements may be made to have a special assistant or aide in the classroom for your child.

Visit the classroom with your child to meet the teacher and classroom assistant before the first day of class. It is a good idea to have any special equipment or appliances that will be brought to the classroom present at the beginning of school, so that all the children can become familiar with them.

Again, the teacher should be there for you as well as for your child. Don't hesitate to share your suggestions and your anxieties. Everyone should be working together to ensure a happy and rewarding year for your child and all the children in the class.

Should I visit the school first—and what should I look for?

Yes! Don't rely on hearsay or reputation, because people have different priorities and may select a school based on any number of reasons that have little to do with your own priorities. By visiting the school yourself, you will get a gut feeling about the atmosphere of each school.

Visit the first time without your child. This will enable you to focus on your own feelings without trying to see the school through your child's eyes. Also, by going alone, you won't have to be concerned about how your child is reacting or behaving.

It's proper to call and make an appointment with the school office for a formal visit. I would suggest, however, that you drop in one morning unannounced, take a walk through, assess your first impression, then make formal appointments with the schools you liked.

Questions to Ask Yourself When Previewing a School

★ Does the school look and feel welcoming?
★ Are the rooms bright, clean, and cheery?
★ Do the children look relaxed and happy?
★ Are the teachers and assistants smiling?
★ Do you hear the busy hum of happy children?
★ Do you see children's artwork displayed?
★ And most important, can you imagine your child being happy here?

If the answer to these questions is yes, this is a school worth considering. You can then make a formal appointment to meet with the school's director.

How can I assess a school's health and safety?

Safety should be the primary concern of any preschool director. Licensing by state or local governing agencies and accreditation by the National Association for the Education of

Young Children (see question 8) are the best assurances that the school meets regulated standards of safety. You may also ask about safety standards, such as:

★ *First aid qualifications of staff members.* Are staff members certified in infant and child first aid and CPR?

★ *Security procedures.* Are all outside doors securely locked during school hours? Are all visitors met and escorted by a staff or custodial staff member?

★ *Street and parking lot safety.* Are all play areas safely away from traffic and parking? Are children escorted to and from cars by an adult?

★ *Safety precautions with toys and play equipment.* Are all toys clean and in good condition? Does the playground look safe, with a soft surface ground cover? Does the playground meet the safety standards of the U.S. Consumer Product Safety Commission? Ask. Are staff members trained to be watchful while children are at play? See also question 57.

★ *Regular safety evaluations.* Are there regular fire drills and safety inspections by state and local inspectors? Are exits clearly marked? Is a safety inspection certificate displayed?

★ *Acceptable teacher/child ratio.* The National Association for the Education of Young Children recommends one adult for every four to six two-year-olds, one adult for every seven to ten three-year-olds, and

one adult for every eight to ten four-year-olds. Needless to say, the fewer children, the better.

★ *Safety and health education.* Are children taught how to use toys and equipment in a safe manner? Do staff and children practice frequent hand washing? Are disposable gloves used by staff during diaper changes, and are changing areas disinfected after each use? Is nutritious food served at school, and are children educated about the value of good eating habits? Are emergency numbers posted by office telephones? Are parents educated about when to keep sick children home?

Parents need assurance of their children's physical and— less tangible but just as important—emotional and sexual safety. In a school situation, this can be achieved by considering only those schools that have an open-door policy. Parents should feel free to drop in unannounced anytime. If you see anything that you feel is unsafe, or you have questions or concerns about school safety, speak with the director of your child's school. Everyone has the same goal—to maintain a safe and healthy environment for the children.

What does the director do?

The director of a preschool is the person who sets the tone for the entire school. She hires and supervises the staff and oversees every single aspect of running and managing the school. Some of the director's duties include handling all matters related to policies of admission and enrollment, school educational goals, continuing education, school board, fiscal budget, health and safety, programming, and general troubleshooting.

Despite all these responsibilities, a good director will be accessible to both staff and parent to listen and respond to questions and concerns. The director is there for you. Do not hesitate to avail yourself of the director's expertise and guidance. Do try to phone ahead for an appointment to talk, but you can always stop in and ask if she is available to talk for a few minutes.

What questions should I ask the director?

Before enrolling your child, you should feel free to ask the director about anything that hasn't been addressed by the teacher or the school's orientation materials or brochure, such as:

★ Whether there is a written overview of the school's philosophy.

★ Whether the school is licensed or accredited. (See question 8.)

★ School hours. Is an extended-day program available?

★ Teacher/child ratio. Be sure the numbers quoted do not include resource people, such as music teachers, art teachers, or movement teachers, who may come only once a week. (See question 13.)

★ The school's philosophy on discipline.

★ Safety and health policies. (See question 13.)

★ Toileting policy. May diapered children attend? (See questions 38 and 39.)

★ Staff qualifications. Does every teacher have a degree or training in early childhood education?

★ Whether activities such as free play, arts and crafts, books, music, science, playground, and creative movement are integrated into the daily curriculum.

★ How academically oriented the program is.

★ Whether a summer program is offered.

★ How are payments structured? Must payment be made yearly, by semester, monthly, or according to a flexible payment plan? Is financial aid available?

★ When you need to register. (See question 6.)

★ Whether you and your child may visit the classroom(s). (See question 19.)

What's best for my child— a half-day, full-day, or extended-day program?

The choice of how many hours and how many days to send your child to preschool depends on many factors. Some schools make the decision for you. For instance, a school with a three-hour day might have two-year-olds attend two mornings, three-year-olds attend three mornings, and four-year-olds attend five mornings. Other schools offer a choice. For example, two-year-olds may attend two or three mornings, three-year-olds may attend three or five mornings, and four-year-olds may attend five mornings with an option to attend afternoon sessions as well.

Sound overwhelming? Let's make it easy. As long as a program is developmentally appropriate to the age of your child, the number of hours and days become less important. After you have considered your child's readiness (see question 4), you need to evaluate your own priorities. Can you bear to part with your little one for more than two mornings? Or do you need five mornings for yourself? Are you working and figuring out the logistics of who will pick your child up after school? You should be able to find a program that will be good for your child and will at the same time meet your needs.

Why do some schools do admissions testing?

Thankfully, most schools accept children on a first-come, first-served basis, or base acceptance on maintaining a gender balance in each class. Some preschools, usually those in large cities, do screen applicants to assess a child's readiness for school, academic ability, and achievement level. Sometimes a family's financial, ethnic, or religious background is considered in order to maintain a balance in the school's population.

In addition to a general screening, more selective schools conduct comprehensive interviews with the parents. The child is usually interviewed separately, although some schools allow parents to sit quietly by while their child is being interviewed and tested. Some schools will merely observe a child at play with a few other children in order to assess language, socialization, and play skills. Other schools require more formal testing to gauge verbal-skill age, gross and fine motor control, problem-solving skills, confidence, frustration handling, and general intelligence and personality.

If the school you have selected does require admissions testing, keep in mind that the school is not looking for geniuses or prodigies. Schools really do want a population of mixed-ability children who bring with them a variety of aptitudes and talents. Never put pressure on a child before test-

ing. Prepare your child by telling her that she will be going to play games and talk with a teacher at a school that she might like to go to. Find out ahead of time if you will be allowed in the room during testing. If not, tell your child that you will be waiting right outside the room while she plays, and that afterward you will both go for a special lunch or treat. Try to keep the whole admissions and testing process in proper perspective. Your child is who she is, and if one school doesn't accept her on the basis of its testing, there will be another school that will appreciate her for all of her wonderful attributes, and that school will be the right one.

Will my child learn about cultural diversity in school?

If having your child exposed to cultural diversity is important to you, look for a school that includes an anti-bias curriculum. A preschool program that emphasizes diversity promotes respect and consideration for all people regardless of race, religion, family background, social status, and culture. This is demonstrated visually throughout the school by the use of pictures and posters of people of varied racial and ethnic groups. Because recognition and respect for every child's culture and heritage is vital to self-esteem and identity, children need to see dolls, play food, books, and dress-up clothing that reflect their own as well as different cultures. Music and dance from different lands will be presented in a school that appreciates diversity. Foods from different lands will be served and holidays celebrated.

In my own classroom of two- and three-year-olds, we learn to say "Good morning" in fifteen different languages, including sign language. Every morning each child decides in which language he or she will greet the other friends in the circle, and the other children return the greeting. In September, we learn the American greeting, and each week thereafter we learn a greeting from another land. Parents from all cultures are invited to come in and share stories, pictures, music, dress, and food with the children. Photos are taken and displayed. This is enriching for our little ones in an anti-bias curriculum.

My classroom assistant, Sarah, is from Ethiopia. One day, she and I were holding down a piece of paper on a table. One of the children ran to us, looked down at our hands together, and said excitedly, "Look! Doris is vanilla and Sarah is chocolate. You're both delicious!"

Transition to Preschool: Your Child's—and Your— First Days

How can I best prepare my child?

Selecting a preschool seems like an easy task for many parents compared with their worries about how their little ones will handle the separation from Mom and Dad. There are a multitude of theories and methods from the experts concerning separation anxiety. But my experience and perspective from inside the classroom have convinced me that for the vast majority of children, "Less is more." The less focus on the upcoming first day of school, the better. Children never fail to absorb their parents' anxieties, so the less you focus on the impending separation, the easier it will be on both you and your child.

On the other hand, you do need to prepare your child. There are many small things you can and should do months before preschool begins to prepare your child to think of preschool as a happy, friendly, and even familiar place filled with new friends, toys, and adventure. Many months before school, begin using the word *school* in everyday conversations. Read books to your child about preschool. As you are taking walks with your child, point out children on their way to or from school. Talk about friends and relatives who go to school.

You could tell your child that when he gets bigger he may go to school and play. Take your child to visit the school you have selected. Check with the school office about visiting hours. If your child has been assigned to a class or teacher, tell him that you will both be going to visit a school, to see the toys in the school, the teachers, and the children playing in the school.

After getting permission from the office, visit the class for at least fifteen to twenty minutes. Ask if your child may walk around and touch. If the teacher objects, hold your child on your lap and point out all the wonderful toys, posters, art materials, and busy children. You could say, "Doesn't this look like fun! School looks like fun! Maybe you can come back and play here sometime." Make your visits with your child short and sweet.

If your child will be starting school in the fall, make these visits in the spring. That way, when you talk about school all summer, he will be able to recall a happy memory.

If you have been assigned a class and a teacher and have visited, talk about your child's class and teacher by name. It would be nice while you are visiting to take a photo of the room and the teacher so that you can talk about them during the summer.

Don't overdo it! If you talk about it too much, your child will pick up your anxious feelings. Just bring up the subject whenever it seems appropriate. Explaining what to expect to toddlers and preschool age children gives them a sense of predictability and thereby eases the stress of separation.

Around the age of two, most children begin to feel a more pronounced level of comfort about themselves as separate from their parents. Beginning school at this age allows them the opportunity to develop relationships with others besides their parents. It is important long before school begins, however, to allow children to become accustomed to being taken care of by other adults such as extended-family members or babysitters. This exposure enables children to build trusting relationships outside of the immediate family. The underlying message is that parents will always come back, thereby laying the foundation for an easier separation at the beginning of school.

Preparing Your Child for School

★ Begin using the word *school* in everyday conversations.

★ Read books to your child about preschool (see appendix for suggested titles).

★ Point out children on their way to or from school as you are taking walks with your child.

★ Talk about friends and relatives who go to school.

★ Tell your child that when he gets bigger, he may go to school and play.

★ Take your child to visit the school you have selected. Take pictures so you can refer to them in conversations you have with your child about preschool.

★ Talk about your child's class and teacher by name.

★ Don't overdo it! Your child will pick up on your anxious feelings.

Why is a children's orientation program important?

How wonderful it is when a child can begin school feeling comfortable and familiar with his or her teachers and classroom! Visiting ahead of time will enable your child to come back feeling ready to stay and play. A week before school begins, the parents and child should be scheduled to visit the classroom.

I schedule just one child, parent, and room staff to come for a quiet introductory twenty-minute visit to the classroom. I set up the room as I would do for a regular school day—Play-Doh on a table, puzzles and manipulative toys on another table, easel and paints ready, blocks spilled on the floor, dolls and play animals out, kitchen play corner ready, and lights on.

When the child comes to the door with the parent, I stoop down to the child's level and say softly, "Hi, Joshua, I'm Teacher Doris and this is your Puppy Room. Come on in and see all the toys." I then back away and allow the parent and child to look around. I join them, pointing out the things that I perceive the child to be interested in. I keep my voice quiet and my body low, and I try to bond with the child in these first few minutes. As soon as the child is absorbed in play, I call the classroom assistant over and introduce her so that she can meet the child.

I then take the opportunity to invite the parent to sit down with me and I ask, "What would you like us to know about Joshua?" This allows parents to share any anxieties they may have about their child.

I make time to go back and play with the child. At the same time, I observe personality—for example, quiet, shy or extroverted. I also observe verbal-skill level. It is quite normal and expected at this first visit for some or most children to be cautious and restrained. That's okay. The mission of getting acquainted is still being accomplished—on their terms—in a way that's comfortable for them.

I will then say, "It's time for us to say goodbye now. All the toys will be here next time. Will you come back and play another day?" Most children will be absorbed in play and won't want to go. I tell the parent that it's good for the child to leave wanting more and I advise the parent to pick the child up even if she's crying, and leave, promising that she will come back and play some more another day. I tell the child that the next time they come, there will be other friends to play with. We wave a cheery goodbye and I greet the next child and parent.

For the first few weeks of school, we are on an abbreviated schedule: we meet for two hours instead of the regular three hours. When we feel the class has settled in, we begin our full morning schedule (9 A.M. to 12 noon). This usually happens within the first few weeks. Remember, the children are only going two or three times a week. They don't feel the continuity of going every day, so working up to full schedule can take a while.

The first days of school we invite half the class (usually six children) at a time, thereby allowing the staff members to

give each child individual attention. The entire class comes the third session.

Every preschool has an orientation program. Some schools do begin a full schedule immediately and report success. Ask your child's school about its orientation program. If the entire class is expected to meet the very first day and you are not comfortable with that, you can certainly ask if you and your child may have a quiet visit before school begins.

How can I help my child separate?

Helping your child to separate successfully from you should begin long before preschool. Playing the peek-a-boo game with your infant is setting the stage for successful separation later. When you leave your toddler for a moment to get something from the next room and you say, "Mommy (or Daddy) will be right back," you are setting the stage for successful separation, especially if you exclaim, "See? Mommy (or Daddy) came back," when you return (a mantra that will often be repeated in the first days of school). If you are a working parent, sometimes saying the "Mommy always comes back" statement upon returning home is a good idea. Once again, don't overdo it. Keep it light and sporadic.

We need to be careful about projecting our own anxieties onto our preschoolers. Sometimes sending our child off to school for the first time reawakens in us long-forgotten feelings of fear, abandonment, and helplessness. We all went to school for the first time; now it's your child's turn to have that experience. But remember, he will not experience it the same way you did. Your child is lucky to have you for a parent—someone who is concerned enough to prepare him for school and support him every step of the way. If feelings of anxiety do emerge in your child, remember to smile and give lots of hugs, and both of you will feel better.

When you and your child visit the school, you can point out that the children are playing for a little while, then the mommies or daddies or nannies come back to take them home.

Another good idea is to arrange a few play dates with another child in the class, preferably in your own neighborhood. The teacher ought to be able to provide you with the class list. Having a friend in class sometimes eases the separation from a parent. Reading a book once in a while about beginning preschool is helpful if the book gives a happy overview of a morning in school and ends with the children going home.

A day or so before school begins, tell your child that he will go to play in school for a while and that you will be waiting for him with a big hug when school finishes. On the first day remind him that he is going to play in school with the teacher and the other children, and that you will be back to give hugs and kisses and to take him home. Always remember to tell your child in the morning who will be picking him up. Preparing your child prevents unhappy surprises and tears when a babysitter appears instead of you to take your tired little one home. Whenever you talk with your child about school, remember your child is not only listening to your words, he is watching you and sensing your feelings about this new situation. Try to keep your tone reassuring and light.

Easing the Separation Process

★ Tell your child that you love him and that you will be back to take him home right after playground (or whatever the last activity is). This reinforces not only that you will return, but also at what time (events are more meaningful markers of time to young children than hours).

★ *Smile* as you leave. This shows your child that you feel good about leaving her in this wonderful place.

★ Ask you child if he would like to say goodbye while he is playing with the puzzle or if he would rather walk you to the door to say goodbye. This gives your child a measure of control.

★ Ask your child where she would like her goodbye kiss. On her nose? On her elbow? Plant the kiss with a quick goodbye, making it silly so you leave while you're both giggling.

★ Always alert the teacher when you are ready to leave so she can move right in to distract your child with conversation and play.

★ If your child had trouble separating the first day, leave *one* of your possessions with him. Parents have left sets of old car keys, an extra purse

containing some of Mommy's things, a photo of the family (preferably laminated), a note saying that you will be back at twelve for the teacher to read as often as needed, Daddy's tie, Mommy's scarf, or anything that you think will be meaningful to your child.

What if my child cries the first day?

Many children cry for a few minutes upon separating from the parent the first day or the first few days of school. Your child's teacher and classroom assistants are ready for this. They will be gentle and reassuring to the crying child. They will try to get him involved in a book or toy while holding him and speaking softly. Remember, your child already began to bond with the teacher and classroom assistants on visiting day. There are so many exciting things to see and do in a preschool classroom that most children are able to be distracted in a very few minutes and are ready to play.

Teachers are trained in early childhood development and therefore have an understanding of separation issues for children of this age. A phrase that is heard many times the first few days of school is "Mommies and daddies always come back!"

Many times the first day of preschool is much more difficult for the parent than for the child. Our school has a tea-and-sympathy room staffed by veteran parents who have already been through the angst of separation in previous years and are there to provide a sympathetic ear and tissues for the first-time parent. Parents are welcome to wait in school for the first day or subsequent days, if they wish. The teachers drop in to the T&S room to let the parents know how things are going in their child's classroom.

You certainly should ask what special arrangements your school has made for parents during the first days of orientation.

How long should I continue to try if my child cries every time?

I am the mother of a preschool dropout. When my youngest son was almost three years old, I enrolled him in a neighborhood preschool that came highly recommended. Every school day for almost two weeks, I peeked through the school window to see (and hear) my beloved son standing in the middle of the floor crying. No one came to comfort him. No one came to hold him and tell him everything was going to be all right. The pain I felt watching him was unbearable, but I was too shy to confront the teacher. I took him out of that school and for the rest of the year he played at home. The next year when he was four, he skipped happily into a better preschool. That experience changed my life.

So at the first parents' room meeting every September, I tell parents attending that I wear two hats. One is a teacher's hat; the second is a mother's hat. I truly understand the pain of watching a child cry because he wants you. I understand and remember all too well the feelings of guilt and frustration and helplessness. The children in my class are held, comforted, and soothed when they need it. The parents are held, comforted, and soothed when they need it, too. I counsel the parents to be forever vigilant with every teacher and every school program in which their child is involved. A parent's gut feeling is always correct. If something doesn't feel right, do something about it. Ask questions and demand answers. I wish I had.

If, months after school begins, despite your best efforts, your child cries every time you bring her to school, it's time to take a hard look at your child's unhappiness in the situation. It is up to you and the teacher to figure out the reasons for the unhappiness. There may be several possibilities:

★ The child may not be developmentally or emotionally ready for school. Solution: Keep the child home until the next year.

★ The child may be unable to separate from you. Solution: Stay in school with the child for as long as it takes.

★ This may be the wrong school for your child. Solution: Find a different school with a different "feel."

Your priority should be the happiness and well-being of your child. Even if all your friends' two-year-olds are attending preschool, it's wrong for your child if the experience is not satisfying.

Most two- and three-year-olds are intellectually and developmentally ready for the experience of preschool. Problems arise when a child is not yet emotionally ready to undergo this experience alone. In other words, they are not yet ready to separate from the parent or caregiver. They really want to touch and play with the wonderful toys. They want to experiment with paints and art materials. They want to sing songs with the other children. They want to do it all, as long as Mommy or Daddy is in the same room.

The school you have chosen should have teachers who are flexible and willing to work with the parents of such children. Keep in mind that there are no magic techniques that work for every problem or every child. Fortunately, there are many techniques to try before removing the child from school. You certainly should ask your child's teacher for her suggestions, and you may suggest some additional ideas, such as:

1. GRADUAL SEPARATION

With the teacher's permission, simply stay as long as your child needs you there. If neither parent can take off from work, someone else—Grandma, a child-care provider, a favorite neighbor—may be able to stay. Some children need ready access to a parent or parent figure many times during the morning until the transition to school is successful. It's worth the effort.

You should sit in a chair against a wall in the room looking as inconspicuous as possible. Bring a book, needlework, or writing materials to make yourself as busy as possible, interacting with the child only when approached. You are there for support, not as a playmate.

Usually after the third or fourth day, your child has gotten into the routine of the school morning, is enjoying the school experience, and is ready for you to leave the room for a few minutes. Tell the child that you are going to the bathroom and will be right back. Coordinate the timing with the teacher so that she can move right in to distract the child. When you return, be sure to exclaim, "See, I came back!" This is a weaning process and may take several school days to succeed. Because every child is unique, the process may take more or less time, but it is time worth investing.

2. SHORTER MORNINGS

The child may be brought to school a half hour after the other children arrive, when it is more likely that no one else is crying and the teacher will be available to give your child 100 percent of her attention.

Assure your child that you will return, then leave. In another area of the building, wait an hour, then reenter the room and tell the child that it is time to leave. If the child has been crying intermittently, she should now understand that you are indeed coming back for her. She will feel secure enough to try again another day.

If, after the hour, your child has settled in and appears to be calm, you have the option of taking her home anyway

with happy thoughts of school. Or you could wait in the hallway, unobtrusively peeking in through the door, ready to swoop in at the first look of distress on your child's face. The message to the child is the same, "Mommy or Daddy will always come back." The child will surely feel more secure next time.

3. LATER ENTRY

Sometimes, if all else fails, the solution is to remove the child temporarily from school and try again in two or three months. Your child could be told something like, "The other children are having fun in school, and when you are feeling a little bigger, maybe you can come back and play." No recrimination, no guilt—just a positive statement. Play dates at home could be arranged with children from the class, so that when your child returns to school, friendships will have been formed.

Every teacher of two- and three-year-olds has her own creative repertoire of successful techniques. Don't be shy about asking for suggestions. Some teachers suggest that parents leave a personal item with their child—an extra set of keys, an old wallet, or a scarf (especially one that smells like Mom), so that the child will have something tangible to hold on to as a reminder that Mom or Dad will come back. A family photo is another good idea. I sometimes ask Mom to write a special note to her child to be carried around and read over and over again when reassurance is needed. With everyone involved working together, a successful and satisfactory separation can be accomplished.

How should the first days of school be handled?

You will probably be given a school manual or attend a preschool meeting that will outline the school's policy regarding the adjustment period for new preschoolers. Many programs encourage parents or caregivers to bring the children into the classroom and stay and play for all or part of the first days of school. Other programs encourage parents or caregivers to bring the children into the classroom, play for a few minutes, and then say goodbye and leave. Either way, your child should be encouraged to explore and interact with the other children and adults in the classroom.

When you do feel that it is time to leave, always tell your child. Never sneak away. Give hugs and kisses, and tell her that you will be back to bring her home soon. Alert the teacher, then leave with a confident smile. The teacher will step right in and play with your child. Remember, those who hesitate are lost. If your child senses your ambivalence, she may cry.

How will other children react to a special-needs child?

Each year for the past ten years, I have been fortunate enough to have at least one child in my class with an identi-

fied special need, including PDD (pervasive developmental delay), autism, deafness, and cerebral palsy. I tell the parents of the child with a special need that I consider it a privilege to have their child in my class. Furthermore, the other children in the class are lucky to be able to know their child. Not only are the other children educated in the needs of the special child, but they also have a unique opportunity to learn to be giving, caring, nurturing, and patient (when needed), and most important, to learn that a child with special needs is more like them than different. A friend is a friend.

One year, we all learned sign language so we could communicate with Brian, a wonderful boy with laughing eyes who was deaf. A letter was sent home to all of the parents alerting them that if they observed their children making unusual motions with arms and fingers, that was the new language we were learning in class. It worked beautifully. The children learned to communicate nonverbally and to listen with their eyes as well as their ears. It was a good year for everyone.

We had a disruptive child one year who could not pay quiet attention and instead would make loud vocalizations when everyone else was at circle. The other two-and-a-half-year-olds would invariably say, "That's okay, Adam isn't ready to sit like we do. Maybe he will when he's a little bigger"—parroting what they had heard me say at the beginning of the school year. The children knew that although the toys were put away, it was all right that Adam played with them away from the circle. We knew that he was listening and learning while he played, even though he wouldn't sit with us. Imagine—two-and-a-half-year-olds with so much under-standing and acceptance!

When we had a child with physical challenges, like the beautiful Amy with cerebral palsy, every child wanted to sit beside her on the floor to help balance her. The children took turns for the privilege. Amy always rewarded them with a beaming smile and happy wiggles. When she first tried to use a walker, the other children stood before her a few feet away and, with outstretched arms, shouted words of encour-agement for every leg movement. All the adults were smiling with tears in their eyes. That is the privilege of having a child with special needs in a class.

As inclusion becomes more and more prevalent, one hopes that the attitudes of teachers, fellow students, and parents will be not only welcoming but appreciative as well.

What does a parents' organization do?

Many preschools have active parents' organizations to sup-port and improve the school. Some do fundraising for the school, while others take an active role in developing a sense of community among school families. This is done through socials, carnivals and fairs, and educational programs. Pre-schools with affiliations may have parents' organizations that help sponsor activities for the children around holiday time.

All school parents' organizations welcome volunteers. Parents may volunteer to help as much or as little as they like. Some activities need people during the school day, while

others need volunteers to attend planning sessions or activities in the evening or on weekends.

Volunteering to be part of a parents' organization is also an excellent way for you to meet people and make friends. Whether you are a working parent or an at-home parent, your time and support for this type of organization is beneficial to your child, the school, and you. If your child's school does not have this type of organization or does not want one, you might ask the director if there are ways in which you can be involved and helpful to the school.

Will there be an introductory parents' meeting before school begins?

All parents have questions and anxieties about sending their child to school for the first time. Orientation meetings are when the school apprises parents of the general workings of the school. Handbooks and calendars may be distributed at that time. If there is a parents' organization or support committee for the school, representatives may speak about opportunities for parental involvement. There may be an opportunity to ask questions and have them answered. In addition, some schools actually have a room meeting, where all of the parents meet with their children's teacher in the classroom for a more informal orientation.

Ask whether the school you have chosen schedules a before-school parent-orientation meeting. Your questions

and anxieties are important and need to be addressed. You might ask questions about help in getting a car pool started. Does the school provide a roster with addresses? Don't feel bashful about asking questions. Anything in this book is appropriate to ask about.

What You and Your Child's Teacher Should Know About Each Other

Will the teacher show affection for my child?

Nobody loves your child as you do. Preschool teachers, however, chose their career because they really love young children. Furthermore, they enjoy being with young children, large numbers of them. This dedicated and educated group of teachers comes equipped with humor, energy, developmental expertise, sensitivity, patience, and a capacity for giving and receiving affection. And they are there every day, waiting for your child.

Each year for twenty-five years I have fallen in love with the children in my class. Every year I think that this is the most wonderful group of children in the world and that I will never be as fond of another group of children. And voilà, the next year I am in love again!

I have been deeply saddened in recent years to witness how a handful of nationally publicized cases of sexual-abuse allegations in day-care centers have caused teachers to be wary of expressing affection to young children in their charge. Hugs are a vital part of a preschool program and should be dispensed PRN (a pharmacist's term meaning "dispense as needed"). Teachers of young children should feel free to administer a hug whenever they feel it is appropriate without having to worry whether their sign of affection or comfort may be misconstrued as improper. We teachers are viewed as surrogate parents by the children in our care, and the smiles and hugs we give are far more important than a hundred shiny new toys.

What should I expect from the teacher?

Preschool teachers are hired for their ability to provide warmth, nurturing, respect, and acceptance of each child as an individual. They are trained to facilitate programs of learning that promote social, physical, emotional, and cognitive growth—all in a morning or afternoon of good-natured fun.

In addition, head teachers should have a degree in early childhood education, and all supporting staff should be trained in early childhood education and development. While the teacher provides warmth and nurturing, she should also be able to set firm limits and lovingly enforce them. All staff should be responsive to children by speaking with them at their eye level in warm conversational tones. Teaching staff should encourage children to verbalize feelings and ideas and be quick to step in to help children deal with anger and frustration. Staff should foster independence in children by teaching skills such as personal cleanliness, picking up toys, and caring for personal possessions and classroom materials, along with general self-help skills. Teachers should create a relaxed atmosphere in which children can play and learn.

A tall order? Perhaps. But you have every right to expect

all this for your child. In addition, you should expect a free and easy flow of information about your child from the teacher whenever you feel the need for it. If you think your child's teacher is lacking the above attributes, by all means bring this to the attention of the school director. Your child deserves the best.

Will the teacher watch my child as closely as I do?

The real question is, Will she protect him from getting hurt, getting hit, or feeling sad? You need to be certain that the school you have selected has an appropriate teacher/child ratio. The National Association for the Education of Young Children recommends one adult for every four to six two-year-olds and one adult for every seven to ten three-year-olds. You certainly do not want a teacher hovering over your child. Each child should learn to feel independent and self-reliant. And although no one will watch your child as closely as you do, preschool teachers and classroom assistants are trained to watch and listen for anything untoward happening. Or about to happen.

The teachers are also watching to make sure that every child is occupied and happy. They are observing body language and facial expressions and are always ready to offer reassurance and comfort when needed.

How often can I talk with my child's teacher?

You should be able to talk with your child's teacher as often as you wish. Because you are partners in your child's education, communication is crucial. You certainly can't expect a full conference about your child every time you see the teacher. You can, however, expect to have general questions answered, such as, "How did he do today?" or "Any problems?"

Anytime you have a question, a concern, or some information about your child, such as something happening at home that is affecting your child, always ask to speak with the teacher. She may make time after school or may prefer to be called at home. Ask.

Can I expect formal conferences?

Scheduled conferences with your child's teacher should be held at least once a year to discuss your child's progress and accomplishments and any concerns by either the parents or teachers. These conferences do not take the place of daily informal communication but provide the opportunity for parents to ask questions, voice concerns, and perhaps make suggestions about their child or the school's program.

Of course, you should expect to be able to confer with

your child's teacher anytime you feel the need, but the scheduled conference will give you a more detailed view of how your child is doing in school. It is not unusual for parents to bring a list of questions, which the teacher will be happy to address. In all likelihood, the teacher will have a predetermined agenda for the conference.

I like to describe to the parents the entire morning's schedule and inform them specifically about how their child reacts to and participates in each activity. I relate personal anecdotes about their child and take the opportunity to describe behaviors that may be of concern, or more often, delight. I tell parents that there will be time for questions after my presentation but they should feel free to jump in anytime with questions. Whenever either Mom or Dad has been unable to attend, some attending parents have brought tape recorders to record their child's first conference. The absent parent can then listen at home to what was said.

It has been my experience that year after year parents always want to know who their child is playing with. I explain that, typically, two-year-olds don't play with any one child in particular. They engage in parallel play. That is to say, whoever happens to be next to them at the sand table is who they are playing with—for the moment. Whoever is in the rocking boat with them is who they are playing with—for that moment. Close friendships are usually not formed until the age of three or beyond. I frequently observe children in my three-year-old class "pairing up." I always send a note home to the parents so they may arrange after-school play dates.

Another frequently asked question is, "How is his behavior

at school? Because he is really misbehaving at home lately."
Parents are surprised to learn that little Joey is a model of
compliance at school. I explain that while in school, children
are giving 110 percent in effort. There are new rules to learn.
There are new limits. There is a new schedule. So much to
learn and remember! Small wonder that when two-year-old
Joey is home, he is so comfortable that he lets his guard
down completely. After a morning of trying to remember all
of the do's and don'ts of functioning in a group, he acts out
at home. Where better than at home, surrounded by the
people who love you no matter what you do? This type of behavior is usually a stage that will pass as school becomes
more of a routine.

During a conference, if you ask a teacher a developmental question to which she doesn't know the answer, ask for
recommended reading on the subject. I personally swear by
Child Behavior: The Classic Child Care Manual from the Gesell
Institute of Human Development, available in most book-
stores (see also Appendix). This perennial favorite describes
every stage of development and behavior of children from
the age of two-and-a-half to ten years. I have copied and sent
home relevant chapters to the parents in my classes, and I
have advised my own children to consider it their bible of
child rearing.

On conference days, many teachers are not only nervous
but hungry and thirsty as well. One very thoughtful parent
who had an early conference appointment brought coffee
and doughnuts! I have never forgotten that act of early-
morning kindness.

Does the school's curriculum live up to my expectations?

If there is a concern that your child is not being challenged or you feel that your child is bored in class, plan to observe your child's class one or more mornings. It is possible that your child's efforts are going toward building social skills, learning to share, experimenting with imaginative play, or a myriad of other experiences that you cannot see or learn from your child after school. If the curriculum continues to fall short of your expectations, certainly bring your concerns to the attention of the teacher.

If the literature you received from your child's school promised a creative movement class once a week, or a music or dance class, and your child tells you that he has not attended such classes, ask the teacher about the discrepancy. Be diplomatic and remember to use the "I" message ("I was told there would be a weekly music class, and Adam says that he has not been to a music class") rather than the more threatening "you" message ("You promised a music class, and Adam said there is none"). It is possible that Adam has been attending music class but is not communicating that to his parents. Perhaps the music teacher has been ill and the classroom teacher has had an informal music session in the classroom. Maybe the school was not able to hire a special music teacher and neglected to inform the parents.

Teachers of two- and three-year-old children are trained not to overstimulate or overburden their little ones with in-

appropriate materials. They are constantly reevaluating the curriculum to ensure that it is geared to the specific interests and abilities of the children in the class. Teachers are generally receptive to constructive suggestions and should be willing to try more challenging materials, if appropriate. Unless there is feedback from the parents, teachers assume everyone is satisfied.

If you have brought a concern to the attention of a teacher and you are dissatisfied with the outcome, speak with the school director.

What if I don't like my child's teacher or one of the classroom aides?

All parents hope and expect to establish a warm relationship with their child's teacher. If you are experiencing negative feelings toward the teacher or a classroom assistant, however, try to be very clear in your own mind about the cause of those feelings. If the reason is obvious—for instance, if you feel that a staff member has been insensitive, negative, or unkind toward you, or worse, your child—it is vital that you bring this problem to the attention of the classroom teacher first. Ask for an informal conference. A teacher is more likely to respond positively to the diplomatic "I": "I was worried when Joey told me that . . ." "I" statements present a thoughtful concern.

The discussion gives the teacher the chance to provide

an explanation for the problem or to clear up a misconception. It may well bring forth an apology for inadvertently hurt feelings. If a problem has been brought to the attention of a teacher and you remain dissatisfied with the outcome, go to the school director. The director is there to listen, make suggestions, and resolve problems.

If you do talk with the director, be specific about your complaint. Be ready to offer examples of behaviors that you find troubling. If you are worried about something going on in the classroom, ask the director to personally observe the teacher during class. Ask the director what remedy she would suggest for the problem. Also ask what you can do to help. Everyone working together will help resolve any problem.

Should the teacher be told about personal/family issues?

When a family experiences changes or finds itself in crisis, children are affected. It is important to inform your child's teacher about whatever is occurring at home that might affect your child. Arrange for a special conference to inform the teacher and plan strategies to help your child while at school. Ask for suggestions on how to handle questions about situations that arise at home. Conferring with the teacher enables both of you to help your child work through the situation while feeling support from the adults at home and at school.

Some children welcome the normal routine of the class-

room and may not want to talk about what is happening at home. In most cases, school may be the stabilizing place when home is not. So whether the change is:

★ New baby

★ Moving

★ New babysitter

★ Serious illness

★ Divorce

★ Family death

the teacher needs to know. Children may not react the way we expect. Some mistakenly feel responsible or guilty for whatever has happened and seek punishment by misbehaving. Anger is sometimes a reaction to feeling small and powerless. Teachers are good at redirecting behavior and helping children work through their feelings at such times.

As difficult as it may seem, disclosing personal information of this sort to your child's teacher is always helpful. Expect these matters to be handled professionally and confidentially. If a child is willing to verbalize what is happening at home, these issues can be dealt with in school either by group discussion, books, dramatic play with puppets or dolls, or a quiet talk alone with the teacher. The teacher may be able to suggest books that can answer your child's questions in ways that the child understands. Early childhood teachers are skilled in listening to elicit feelings and giving necessary hugs and reassurance. Again, the sameness of the school routine provides the stability needed at such times.

When I am told that a grandparent has died, or a pet, or a neighbor, we do a mini-unit on death. If we are fortunate enough that no family experiences a death, we do the unit anyway in the spring. A letter is sent home to the parents explaining exactly what will be presented. The letter states that although the children are far too young to understand the concept of death, what we will be doing is, in essence, "planting the seed" of the idea.

A dead insect is brought into the circle, and all of the children gather around. The insect is placed on a tray in the middle of the circle. The children contemplate it for a few minutes, and then I ask why the insect isn't moving. We listen to everyone's ideas, and inevitably someone will say, "Because it's dead." We theorize about death and listen to everyone's ideas about what dead means. I ask if the insect will move or fly away later. Some children say "no" and some insist that it will. The children are allowed to gently poke and move the dead insect.

Then we do an experiment. I place a cracker and a bottle cap filled with water beside the insect and ask if the insect will need to eat and drink. We watch. Then we go to the playroom downstairs. When we return we check to see if the insect has moved, eaten, or drunk the water. All the children see for themselves that the dead insect's body is not working anymore and cannot be made to work (the irreversibility of death); that it no longer moves, feels hurt, eats, drinks, or has needs or wants (the finality of death—it's dead and will not

be alive again). We discuss the life cycle (all insects, birds, animals, and all other living things have a time to live and a time to die).

We read the book *The Dead Bird,* by Margaret Wise Brown, about a group of children who find a dead bird, examine it, and after a childlike ceremony, bury it. I ask my children if they want to bury the dead insect. They always do, and we go outside, each child carrying a plastic spoon for digging, and we perform a burial. The lesson is a shared experience done at an age-appropriate level. The seed of the death experience has been planted, perhaps to be recalled when needed later.

Research and studies have shown that children need preventive help in understanding the concept of death on both cognitive and emotional levels. Without proper explanation, children are likely to explain it to themselves, sometimes in more frightening ways than we can imagine. The truth is easier to deal with than mistaken beliefs.

What if the teacher expresses a concern about my child's development?

A teacher requesting a conference because of a concern strikes fear in any parent's heart. A parent may imagine hearing about anything from major psychological problems to expulsion. In reality, teachers usually need only to share information about new behaviors observed in school. A teacher may observe a child having tantrums, when none

have been seen before, or a child may suddenly become aggressive, or uncharacteristically quiet and withdrawn. If a normally energetic child seems tired and sluggish, or a normally quiet child becomes loud and aggressive, these are changes in patterns of behavior that need further exploration. There are frequently logical explanations, such as a child's not sleeping well since the new baby came home, or a parent's traveling on business, or a child's simply not feeling well. The teacher and parent will work together to help the child feel comfortable with whatever situation has arisen.

Occasionally, a teacher does have a very real concern about language development or delays in any area of development. Knowing that early intervention is critical, a teacher may communicate this type of concern to a parent and discuss the choices: either waiting and observing further or requesting a professional evaluation.

As frightening as this may seem to parents, most speech and developmental lags usually take care of themselves with time. When professional help is needed, early intervention is important to preserve self-esteem.

If a professional evaluation is suggested, the director of the school will have a directory of developmental specialists. Your child's pediatrician also has a list of specialists. Before talking with or visiting a specialist, have a written list of the reasons for the referral. Ask the teacher to write down her observations and concerns and ask her to give specific examples. Ask her if it is possible for the specialist to observe your child in the classroom if that is requested. A developmental or speech pathologist will probably want to see a child in the classroom with his peers to see how he interacts

and communicates with the other children. After an observation, a conference will be requested with the parents and sometimes with the teacher as well, so that everyone involved with the child can coordinate a unified plan of action.

Each year, I have in my class of two- and three-year-olds at least one child with a language delay. When a parent expresses concern in September, I always advise waiting at least two or three months to see if we observe growth in language. If we are hearing progress in speech and language development (even though it is far behind other children's language), we advise waiting longer. Some children progress at their own rate of speed. The key word is progress. If a child has made no progress from September to December, then it's time to ask for an evaluation. The most important thing that I look for is how the child feels about himself. A child may have a language delay or speech dysfluency, causing other children to keep saying, "What? What did he say?" Or if a child grimaces and has trouble articulating his words, even though that child's speech is at an age-appropriate level, we might ask for an evaluation simply to preserve his self-esteem. A speech pathologist can jump-start speech and language fluency. It is important to intervene at this early age, whatever the problem, so that when children begin grade school, they are equipped with developmentally appropriate skills and intact self-esteem.

"What Is the
School's Policy on . . . ?"

Will diapers be changed at school?

Many schools will not accept children in diapers. In schools that accept diapered children, diapers will certainly be changed. If you are sending a child to school in diapers, be sure to ask about the diaper-changing policy of the school. Ask to make sure that your child's school conforms to state or local licensing regulations or has accreditation from the National Association for the Education of Young Children, which has stringent standards concerning the wearing of disposable protective gloves, vigorous hand washing, and the cleanliness of the diaper-changing areas. You may ask to see the changing areas yourself.

Usually at the beginning of the school year parents are asked to send in diapers and wipes. Some schools have a diaper-changing time built into the morning schedule when all the children are changed. Other schools change diapers as needed. If a child absolutely will not allow anyone outside the family to change a wet diaper, the teacher must be notified. In that case, the parent and teacher can work out a compromise, such as having the parent change the diaper at dismissal time. If a child has a bowel movement while at school, the diaper must be changed and the child cleaned despite protestations from him. He will be talked with in a relaxed, reassuring manner while being changed. The teacher might say something like, "I know you don't want to do this now, but as soon as you are all fresh and clean, we can go

back to our class and play with the new puzzle." Diapering time can and should be pleasant, matter-of-fact, and individualized.

Will the teacher help with toilet training?

When you feel that your child is ready to begin using the potty or toilet, tell the teacher. The teacher will probably ask how you would like her to reinforce the learning process while your child is in school. Any good teacher will be happy to comply with your request for assistance in this important event. Always send extra clothing and underwear during the transition period. The teacher will invite your child to the bathroom many times during the morning. No child should ever be forced to the bathroom "just to try." It makes it seem like a chore rather than a natural function. If everyone is light-hearted and matter-of-fact about the whole thing, the child will eventually be ready to take that big step into underwear.

When a parent tells me that her child is wearing pull-up underwear that day for the first time, I will bend down and say, "That's great. Would you like to tell your friends at circle time?" If the child says no, I know that making a fuss for this child would be counterproductive. I will merely whisper to the child that I will be very happy to take her to the bathroom anytime she wants. And I will be careful to ask privately, every half hour, if she needs to go.

If the child would like to share the important news at circle time, she is invited to do so, and I ask if she would like

everyone to clap for her. Great huzzahs are heard, panties are sometimes shown, and the newly pantied one is the envy of all in the circle. Peer pressure is a great motivator in this case. Everyone aspires to the attention and the personal "show and tell."

Remember, though, accidents always happen. Everyone needs to be positive, maintain a sense of humor, and be supportive—even when a child wants to go back to diapers for a while.

What if my child won't use the toilet at school?

Toilet "training" is complicated enough without introducing a new toilet at a new location—namely, school. It's difficult even for some children to settle into the routine of using the toilet at home. Occasionally, I come across a child who absolutely will not use the toilet at school. We're not talking about the child who will wet or soil his underwear. That child is willing to go but still needs help recognizing when it's time to visit the bathroom. We are talking about the child who holds it in all morning.

Preschool teachers ask many times during the morning, "Who needs to go to the bathroom? Who needs to make pooh? Jamie, do you need to make pee-pee?" We teachers worry when we know that Jamie is wearing Batman underwear but Batman has not yet made an appearance in the school bathroom. A conversation with the parent is a good idea. Many times a parent will say, "Oh, we call him 'the

camel.' Don't worry about it. He'll go when he gets home."
When a parent expresses concern about her child's refusal to
use the toilet at school, however, a plan must be devised.

Here's my first suggestion: The next morning, a few minutes before class, Mom should ask Jamie to show her the
children's bathroom. If Mom can be casual and get Jamie to
use the toilet just that first time, usually that's all it takes. If
it doesn't work before school, it should be tried again after
school. The adults should be very calm and nonchalant during this time. Never force the issue. If Jamie is verbal, certainly ask him why he doesn't go to the bathroom at school.
Share that information with the teacher. Is there something
scary about that bathroom? Is it too noisy, with too many
children? Is he afraid to flush? Is the toilet low enough? Does
he just not have to go?

My second suggestion is to call the pediatrician. If the
doctor isn't concerned, you can relax. We never want to make
a child self-conscious about this natural function or create a
problem, especially in this area. Tell the teacher not to worry
and certainly not to focus on this issue with your child. He
will use the school toilet when he is ready.

How should my child be dressed?

Dress your child for comfort. Fancy dresses and party shoes
are lovely to look at but hardly practical when your little
princess is running, sliding, and rolling around in the wood
chips on the playground. All children should be told that it is

their job to play and have fun and not to worry about getting their clothing dirty. No child should have to get hysterical if paint spills on a shirt. So it follows that all school clothing should be washable. Paint and water spills do occur, so most schools ask for an extra set of clothing from each child to be kept in the classroom.

Elastic. Teachers love elastic, especially on waistbands of pants. Remember, this year your little one will probably become toilet-trained. When a child announces, "I have to go *now*," one-piece jumpsuits or layers and layers of clothing are much too cumbersome.

Smocks should always be available at the easel. Some children refuse to wear a smock and will choose not to paint rather than wear one. Therefore, before school even begins in September, the parents in my class are told that no child will be forced to wear a smock. Asked, yes. Forced, no. So it follows that children should come to school wearing washable and comfortable clothing. They shouldn't have to worry about someone being upset about paint spatters on a shirt. Most children will wear a smock when painting, but if your child is one that refuses, save the special clothing for special occasions—not school. The child's job is to paint with abandon and enjoy the process.

How is discipline handled?

The concept of discipline needs to be separated from the concept of punishment. Children need a clear definition of

what is acceptable conduct and what is unacceptable conduct. They feel secure when they know their limits. Nowhere is this more important than with large groups of very young children.

Early childhood educators are trained to understand the developmental stages of the children in their charge. They recognize that the average two-year-old has rather low impulse control. So when Sarah begins to draw on the wall with crayons, the teacher will probably say something like, "Sarah, walls are not for coloring. Paper is for coloring. I will help you clean the wall and then you can color on paper." The limit was stated firmly and clearly. The teacher told Sarah what was unacceptable and what would be acceptable.

Similarly, if a child is going to hurt another child by hitting or pushing, the teacher might say, "Adam, no hitting! I can't let you hurt Joey. I know you want the truck. You need to use your words. Do you need me to help you tell Joey that you want a turn? Joey, Adam says he would like a turn with the truck when you finish playing with it. Will you give it to him in a few minutes?"

The teacher will then make sure Adam gets his turn and both children will be praised—Joey for sharing and being a good friend, and Adam for using his words and learning how to wait (a difficult task for a young child). Everyone feels good.

Again, the limit was stated clearly. The teacher saw to it that each child's needs were met and that both felt respected. There was no need for punishment. Some teachers use a "time-out" chair for the child who is having difficulty calming down. The child is told to sit for a very few minutes until he or she feels ready to play nicely.

Every teacher has a repertoire of strategies and techniques for these kinds of situations. As children get older and more verbal, they will be encouraged to participate in the process of problem solving.

The concept of discipline and limits, however, needs to be separated from the concept of punishment. If little Michael comes home and tells you that his teacher yelled at him and didn't let him go to the playground, a red flag should go up. This sounds like a punishment. If the teacher didn't mention anything to you, and there was no note about anything untoward happening at school, you need to call the teacher. Using the diplomatic "I," say something like, "I was concerned when Michael told me that he was not allowed on the playground today, and I would like to know what happened." Even if Michael hit someone, or threw sand, the objective of discipline is to teach. The ultimate objective is for every child to have self-discipline someday. So listen to the teacher, and if you feel that she was being too punitive, address that issue with her. Ask if there are some other ways the situation could have been handled whereby Michael could have been helped to handle himself appropriately without being punished and separated from everyone.

Parents need to let teachers know what their expectations are in the area of discipline. Even though teachers are trained in handling these types of situations, some people are, by nature, less patient than others. Some teachers prefer to have a lot of control. When that preference impacts negatively on children, perhaps it's time for that teacher to find a different line of work. Fortunately, this doesn't happen very often.

On the other end of the spectrum are the teachers who are too lax about discipline. Children are allowed to shout at each other, grab, push, and act aggressively rather than assertively. This is almost worse than having a punitive teacher. A teacher who is too passive and unsure, no matter how highly educated, is harmful to children. Without limits, children feel unsafe. They push the boundaries, begging to be stopped. Children need the discipline of operating within clearly defined limits and boundaries. A teacher who is unable to provide these to children needs more training. If you see this in your child's classroom, *run*—do not walk—to the school's director. Describe your observation and ask what she plans to do about the situation. I consider this an emergency—not a medical emergency, but an educational one.

Both of these hypothetical cases are the extreme. The vast majority of preschool teachers are patient, gentle, trustworthy, and well trained. Nevertheless, it behooves all parents to know exactly what is going on in their child's classroom, and that includes how discipline is handled by the teacher and the support staff.

Will I be able to observe my child in class?

Yes. I would be wary of a school or a teacher that prohibits parents from visiting their child's class. Admittedly, at the beginning of the school year, it may take a few weeks for all the children in a class to settle in. During that time, a visit from a parent may cause a renewal of separation anxiety.

After the first few weeks, however, most children have learned to successfully separate and are feeling somewhat autonomous. Our school has an open-door policy, and we encourage parents to drop in for a visit. This policy is explained to the parents before school begins in the fall. The parents are also told that when they visit they may expect one of three typical reactions:

★ They may be given a tour of the classroom and pulled into play by their child.

★ They may be, for the most part, ignored by their child.

★ Their child may cry on this visit and become clingy and irritable. This is the child who may be feeling conflicted about who she is when the parent is on her turf. When she's at home with Mommy and Daddy, she feels little. But at school, she feels big. Now that Mommy or Daddy is here at school, she may become confused about her role.

Parents should be encouraged to try to visit, even for an hour, sometime during the school year. If your child seems upset by your visit and it is not a pleasurable experience for either one of you, leave. You can try again in a few weeks or months.

For most parents, however, the visit is a golden opportunity to see with their own eyes their child in his or her life away from home. For the child, it's an opportunity to show Mom or Dad or Grandma the toy she told you about, the water fountain, or the friend who wears the dinosaur shirt.

You will need to call the school office and ask about the policy on drop-in visits. It's a nice courtesy to tell your child's teacher that you may be dropping in during the next week.

Will there be field trips?

Many parents ask about field trips for the two-year-old class. A field trip for two-year-olds can be beneficial if it is safe, age-appropriate, educational, fun, and short in duration. While the four-year-old class is spending a November morning at the museum measuring a stegosaurus and reinforcing all they learned about dinosaurs, the children in the two-year-old class are busy learning how to share, how to follow directions, and how to satisfactorily function in a group. By the spring, with all these accomplishments mastered, perhaps a field trip may be planned.

In my two- and three-year-old class, I like to start with an easy one. Exploring the environs around the school while looking for signs of spring is a good first field trip. We begin our walking field trip after discussing the wonder of a new spring and what we will be looking for to confirm its arrival.

Before opening the door to the outside, we discuss the importance of holding a partner's hand and following behind the teacher (there is always an adult at the end of the line as well), and the hazards of bolting into the street where there are moving vehicles. We review the stop, look, and listen rule for crossing the street, and off we go. As we walk, we listen for birds and look for flowers, insects, new leaves on trees, and new green grass. We feel the warm spring breeze.

When we arrive at a grassy area away from a busy street, we run races, lie on the grass and watch clouds, and talk about spring. Because little legs get tired and group attentiveness is relatively short, we then line up, hold a partner's hand, review the safety rules of crossing streets, and return to school. This is a simple adventure lasting about twenty minutes, and it is developmentally appropriate, safe, and fun.

If the children as a group have cooperated and have enjoyed the outing, other simple trips may be planned. A walk to a firehouse or simply exploring the neighborhood would be appropriate. I believe bus trips to farms, museums, and other such places, though exciting, are too exhausting for groups of little ones and are best left for the four-year-old class or kindergarten.

Are birthdays celebrated in school?

Every child waits with happy anticipation for his or her birthday to arrive. Birthdays mean parties, presents, excitement, and lots of attention. It is also a time when young children easily get overexcited and overstimulated with all the fuss.

All preschools acknowledge children's birthdays, but they may have different practices concerning how birthdays are celebrated in the classroom. Some schools allow only a birthday song, while others may allow parents to orchestrate an extravaganza in the classroom. Most schools, happily, favor a more balanced and age-appropriate celebration. Check with your school about its policy.

For very young children, it is best to keep this first school party low-key. This can be easily done by offering to bring in a birthday cake or cupcakes and party napkins at snack time. Candles may be lit and everyone can sing "Happy Birthday" to the birthday boy or girl. (Don't forget your camera.) Balloons, blowers, and party favors are best saved for a private party at home. As your child's birthday approaches, you might ask the teacher if it is permissible to bring the special birthday snack that day.

When are gifts for teachers appropriate, and what kinds of gifts should they be?

The most wonderful gift you can give a teacher is your appreciation. If your child is excited about going to school, chances are that the teacher has created a safe and warm environment that is making your child happy. Tell the teacher how much you appreciate what she has done for your child. If you especially like a project that your child brings home, tell the teacher. Teachers spend large amounts of time preparing lesson plans and art projects. They welcome positive comments from parents. When teachers are given that type of reinforcement, it makes them feel appreciated by you, the parent. Appreciation is indeed the gift that every teacher needs and wants.

More tangible gifts are traditionally given at Christmas and Hanukkah time. Sometimes a collection is made by the room parent, and a group gift is presented to the teacher from the entire class. If this is not done, small personal gifts are always appropriate. Do include your child in the selection of a gift for the teacher. The giving then becomes meaningful for the child as well as the recipient. Home-baked cookies or breads prepared by you and your child are always a very welcome gift. Remember to include handmade cards from your child.

If, during the school year, your family goes apple picking, remember to bring some extra for the teacher. When at the beach, have your child find a special shell for the teacher. These small gestures have great meaning for your child as well as his teacher.

At the end of the school year, there may again be a group gift presented to the teacher from all the parents. In addition, if you want to express your thanks and gratitude for a teacher whom you think is remarkable, a small personal gift or letter would be appropriate.

One of my all-time favorite gifts was a framed miniature collection of paintings done by every child in my class that year. A very creative and thoughtful mother secretly asked the other parents to have their children make a painting for me. She then had each of the paintings color-copied and reduced to 2½ by 4 inches. She arranged them, had them matted on a dark-blue background, and placed the matted paintings in a 10-by-18-inch frame. It was a fabulous gift, which was presented at our end-of-the-year class party. It hangs in a place of honor in my family room. I love it.

How Can Parents,
Child-care Providers,
and Family Members
Be Involved?

What should a handbook for parents contain?

Every preschool should distribute a parent handbook before school begins. Usually the handbook contains an introduction and welcoming statement by the director that includes the philosophy and objectives of the school. A handbook can be expected to contain information about most of the following:

- ★ Orientation

- ★ Arrival and dismissal procedures

- ★ A schedule of daily activities

- ★ School's philosophy on discipline

- ★ Home–school communication

- ★ Family participation

- ★ Parents' association

- ★ School hours

- ★ Health rules

- ★ Special celebrations

- ★ Holiday celebrations

- ★ Field trips

★ Car pools and parking-lot safety

★ Inclement weather procedures

★ School closing

★ Nutrition and snack

A school handbook is a valuable reference. If you feel that your child's school handbook is lacking information that you deem helpful, make your suggestions known to the director.

Will there be a regular calendar or newsletter?

Preschools are generally good about keeping parents informed of daily events happening in each classroom. One method is to send home a monthly calendar page with reminders of all sorts: children's birthdays, school closings, holiday events, class trips, snack information, and perhaps areas of interest that are being presented that month. A newsletter most often is a general school or parent-to-parent communication rather than a class communication. It may contain announcements of upcoming school events, notices of fundraising events, and perhaps general school news.

Always take the time to read and post calendars and notices that are sent home. There is always the parent who didn't read the reminder on the calendar to send in the white sock for making puppets, or the parent who brings a child to school only to find the building closed, because no one at home noticed that there was a scheduled closing that day. Keeping yourself well informed as to what is happening at your child's school is important. Do it.

How involved should child-care providers be?

Because so many parents are working full-time, teachers may see nannies, permanent babysitters, or other hired child-care providers (I'll just use the term "nanny" for simplicity's sake) at school more than they see parents. Very often the nanny will bring the child to and from school, in which case it is essential that she be introduced to the teacher and staff the very first day of school.

The problem for teachers is one of confidentiality. Information about a child, especially a problem or concern, should be related directly to a parent. It is helpful for the nanny to be present during the formal conference time with the parents. The nanny typically spends more hours with the child during the day, so it is important for her to hear, along with the parents, how the child is doing in school. Any concerns and suggestions by the teacher or the parents should be shared with the nanny so that everyone can agree on how to implement changes in the best interest of the child.

Parents should make every effort to be present at school for special events, such as their child's birthday party, PTA meetings, school fairs, field trips, and any other school function that is important to their child. Even the most loving nanny is not the same as a mommy or daddy at this important and memorable time in a child's life.

What if my child won't tell me what happens at school?

Every year at back-to-school night, parents lament that their children won't tell them what they do at school. Every parent is curious about how and what their child is doing in school. The teacher can only say things like, "He's doing great! He seems to enjoy everything." Nice to hear but hardly satisfying.

Some parents are lucky enough to have a child who comes home and gives complete and vivid descriptions of everything that happened in school that morning. More likely is the parent who hears "Played" when she asks her child what she did at school that day. Played. That's it? Parents find it reassuring to see with their own eyes what their children are doing in the classroom. If you really want to know what your little one does in school, you have some choices other than playing twenty questions with your child.

★ Visit the classroom and observe for yourself.

★ Peek through the window or door. Door windows are designed for observation by parents or anyone else who wants to look in without disturbing the children.

★ Have someone videotape a morning in your child's class. We videotaped a morning of school and provided copies to parents, who were happy to pay the nominal fee. The children were thrilled to watch themselves, their classroom, their teacher, and their friends. We were told that having the videotape enabled the parents to hear from their children everything they ever wanted to know about a morning in preschool.

★ Have someone compile a photo album.

One year I took photographs of the children at every activity during the day: free play, circle time, the playroom, in the bathroom washing hands, book time, snack time, rest time, playground time, and going-home time. I had the photos color-copied and enlarged to 11 by 14 inches. I added captions and a parents' guide and had the whole thing laminated and spiral-bound. This wonderful photo documentary of our daily schedule now goes home with each child in turn. Using the album as a visual prompt, parents can hear in their children's own words what happens at school, whom they play with, what they do, and what they like.

The Day in the Puppy Room book also helps with separation anxiety. At the beginning of the school year, I ask parents to refer their children again and again to the last page, where parents and nannies are waiting with smiles and open arms to take them home. Children need this reassurance over and over again, especially at the beginning of the school year. They need to know that after all the morning's activities are over, they will indeed go home. Our book of photographs fills the needs of parents and children alike.

What should I do with my child's artwork?

The first impulse when looking at a painting made by your two-year-old is to say, "Beautiful. What is it?"

Your child probably doesn't know. She spent maybe five minutes making the brush with red paint go up and down, the brush with the blue paint go sideways, and the brush with yellow paint go over all the other colors. The result? A brown blob. It wasn't supposed to be anything. Your child intently watched the colors trail from the brush. She saw the colors mix when overlapped, and her arm felt good going up high and down low while painting. Developmentally, your child enjoyed the process of painting without thought of the end product. It was just relaxing and fun.

The nicest thing you can say when presented with one of these early endeavors is, "Wow, look at all those colors! I see blue, red, and yellow over here. I can tell you really had fun painting this. It makes me happy." You will surely be rewarded with a proud smile.

Generally, around the age of three, children may be able to look at their finished product and tell a story about it. At that point you might say, "I love it. Tell me about it." That's so much safer then saying that something looks like a cow only to be told that it's a picture of Grandma. Better ask your child to tell about it before volunteering a guess.

If your child brings home only scribbled artwork, rejoice. That your child is happy with her work is more important than how the end product looks to you. The teacher who encouraged your child's creativity and probably praised the process by which those scribbles were made is to be congratulated. Too many teachers of young children take pride in sending home art projects that look so perfect, no child could possibly have done them without a teacher directing every move. If you ask a child who made her picture, and she answers, "Mrs. Smith," no matter how beautiful it is, you know that your child did not enjoy creating that picture— Mrs. Smith did. It is more appropriate to allow a child to create something that is pleasing to her whether or not it looks like anything specific to you or the teacher. The delight in creating comes from the freedom of being able to select materials and colors and to have the time to produce something satisfying.

So when your friend shows off her little Jennifer's perfect flag picture with every star and stripe in place, smile and be secure in the knowledge that your child's red-white-and-blue scribbled work has enhanced her self-esteem and enabled her to take pride in her own creative work. Being able to do representational art is developmental and will come in time.

Of course, you will be displaying the artwork that comes home. Think of it as your growing and growing and growing collection of prized art. As new pieces come home, others by necessity must be taken down. Many parents store them. One parent bought an under-the-bed type storage box for each of his children and invited them to decorate it. Older pieces of art were lovingly put in the box for storage and carefully weeded out with the child before the next school year.

How can I learn the songs sung in school?

"Sing the monkey song with me, Mommy." What's the monkey song? It's obviously a song learned at school by your little one. You don't know the monkey song. Given the disparate levels of language development in preschool children, you certainly can't depend on your child to teach you the monkey song. How, then, can you learn the songs that are sung in the classroom and loved by your children, so that those songs can be enjoyed at home?

You certainly may ask your child's teacher if she would mind turning on a small tape recorder (that you provide) whenever special songs are sung in the classroom. If your child's school has a special music teacher, the same could be asked of her. Assure the classroom teacher that you will not be judging her voice, that you are not scouting for Broadway, and that this tape will be for family use only.

Taping classroom songs can also be a good fundraiser for the PTA. Ask the school director if a tape and accompanying song sheet may be made available to parents for a small fee.

Should I arrange play dates with other children from school?

A play date is an arranged appointment for a child to play with a classmate when school is not in session. There are two schools of thought about play dates. Some professionals and parents believe that today's children are overprogrammed and overscheduled. The fear is that young children are afforded precious little time to daydream, to invent solitary games, or simply to enjoy "down" time alone with a toy or a book.

For the very young child, play dates may present more problems than pleasure. It is difficult for most two- and three-year-olds to share. When a school friend is invited home to play, and beloved items are touched, the invasion may be resented, and parent intervention may be needed to avert tears and tantrums. Not much fun for anyone.

The other school of thought about play dates is that bringing children together after school helps develop friendships and generates better social skills, such as sharing and taking turns. Play dates may help children feel more secure in preschool by having a connection to a special friend as a result of play dates. Many parents enjoy play dates because it gives them an opportunity to make new friendships themselves.

Commonsense Guidelines for Play Dates

★ Keep in mind that little ones tire easily, so keep the play date short and sweet.

★ One or two play dates a week is enough.

★ One friend at a time for a two-year-old is advisable.

★ If your child is playing host, put all special and beloved toys away until the guest goes home.

★ SUPERVISE. Be prepared to deal with conflict and call the play date to an end if either child seems cranky, unhappy, or tired.

★ If your child changes his mind before the play date, call it off. He has a right to change his mind. The other child's parent will understand. You can reschedule for another day.

Safety and
Illness

Will my child need a medical checkup before school?

Yes. Every child enrolled in school needs to bring a pre-admission health-history report and a medical report from a physician. The school will provide the needed forms and the parents have only to take their child for a medical checkup. The pediatrician will then complete the forms, which state that the child is free of communicable disease, has completed necessary immunizations, and is healthy enough to participate in a preschool program.

This information will be given to every parent who registers a child for school. No child will be admitted to school without completion of these forms. Needless to say, it is vital to give complete and truthful information about your child. All information disclosed about health, past and present, is strictly confidential. Special health problems or concerns should be discussed with the school's director and your child's teacher.

What if my child gets hurt at school?

We are talking about "boo-boos," not major emergencies. If a child falls and skins a knee, the site will be washed, a bandage applied, and a magic kiss bestowed. Sand in the eyes,

scratches, bumps, superficial bites, ruffled feelings, and any other minor hurt that occurs in school will be taken care of promptly and lovingly.

Parents should always be notified in writing. Be sure that the school you choose has the policy of notifying parents of all accidents—even minor ones. Sometimes a bruise or redness may appear hours later, so it is essential that parents be informed of all accidents.

How are medical emergencies handled?

The most commonly seen injuries in preschool are bumps, bruises, scratches, and hurt feelings, most of which can be cured by soap and water and a "magic kiss." But schools are also prepared for medical emergencies.

The health, safety, and well-being of every child is the highest priority of every preschool. Before enrolling a child, parents should take the time and effort to check that the school is fully prepared for any emergency. At the very minimum, the school should have a complete and up-to-date first-aid kit as well as personnel trained in first aid and CPR. Each child's emergency telephone number should be posted by the office telephone. Allergy information as well as other essential health information should also be conspicuously posted for all to see.

Included in the registration packet should be an emergency form that will, at minimum, ask:

★ Parents' telephone numbers both at home and at work

★ Person to contact if neither parent is available

★ Child's pediatrician's name and number

★ Child's dentist's name and number

★ Preferred hospital

Also included will be a form authorizing the school to obtain emergency treatment in the event parents cannot be contacted. There will be a health questionnaire about chronic conditions, allergies, past history, and any other information necessary and useful in case of emergency.

Parents should be notified in the event of an incident. Notes home should contain information as to what happened, where and when it happened, and what was done by the teacher. School offices also keep copies of incident reports. Parents should be telephoned if there is a question of bleeding that is not immediately stopped (in case stitches are required on a cut), or for any reason deemed necessary by the teacher or director.

Does the school have a safe, supervised playground?

Every preschool has an outdoor playground, and it is essential that the playground be safe for children. There are certain criteria that should be followed in order to ensure that safety.

Parents may be sure that the playground in a licensed and accredited preschool has met the criteria for high quality and has, in addition, followed the U.S. Consumer Product Safety Commission's established guidelines for safety. Some of the many criteria are:

★ All playground equipment should be sturdy and anchored firmly in concrete beneath the ground.

★ The entire play area should be covered with an impact-absorbent material such as mulch, soft earth, or rubberized padding. (Falls from playground equipment onto hard surfaces are one of the leading causes of injuries.)

★ Screws and bolts must be covered to prevent rust or injury from rough edges.

★ All wood should be treated to prevent rotting and should be reinspected regularly.

★ Metal equipment should be treated to prevent it from rusting.

★ Swings should be securely fastened and made of rubber or other soft material to prevent injury.

★ All ropes and netting should be anchored at both ends.

★ Spaces between ladder rungs should be either smaller than a child's head size or large enough for a child's head to clear without becoming trapped.

Consider only schools that have conformed to these guidelines.

Each individual school has latitude to select from a huge variety of outdoor play equipment. Selections are made according to the ages and developmental needs of the children who will be playing there. There will probably be equipment for climbing, swinging, rocking, and balancing. There will be areas for quiet play as well. Sandboxes, grassy areas, and playhouses invite imaginative play.

Teachers and assistants should supervise children on the playground at all times. The primary function of the adults is to ensure the safety of every child playing outdoors. An adult will probably be stationed at climbing equipment, swings, or any other equipment where children may need assistance. Other staff members should circulate around the playground to facilitate play and assist children who may need some direction and guidance.

Playground time is one of the most important times of the day. All children love it because it provides the opportunity for movement, freedom, exploration, and discovery.

What is the school's policy about contagious illnesses?

There is a growing awareness of the ease with which many contagious illnesses spread in groups of children. Every preschool should issue a parent's handbook that contains guidelines concerning health and illness.

Despite the best efforts of parents and school staff, con-

tagious illnesses continue to occur in the classroom. Schools require notification if a child has chicken pox, head lice, flu, or any other contagious condition. Notices will be sent home to the other parents of the children in that class. Chicken pox is thought to be contagious one or two days before the first bump appears, so it is difficult to prevent contagion. With the advent of the chicken pox vaccine, this highly contagious disease should no longer be a problem in a few years.

Those pesky head lice that sometimes seem to jump from head to head in groups of children are annoying but not serious. Parents should be notified if there is a case of head lice in the class. Some preschools prohibit the use of fabric hats in the dress-up corner, hoping to prevent the spread of lice.

If a child develops signs of flu after class, it is thoughtful to notify the school so other parents can be told to watch for signs of illness in their children. As with any illness, always check with your child's pediatrician for instructions on medication, care, and, after a contagious illness, permission to return to school.

How do I decide whether my child is too ill to attend school?

Children should be kept home if they have:

★ Contagious illness (obviously)

★ Fever

★ Diarrhea

★ Frequent coughing

★ Vomiting

★ Eye infection

★ Colored discharge from the nose

If your child has none of these symptoms but was up most of the night with vague complaints, it is probably better to keep him home. An overtired and cranky child is not going to have a happy and productive school experience in the morning. If a child appears ill at school, the parents will be called to take the child home.

Sometimes deciding whether or not to send your little one to school is a judgment call. Better to err on the side of caution and keep him home.

Will medication be administered if needed at school?

If your child takes medication on a regular basis, this is an important question to ask before enrolling your child in preschool. Most schools will administer prescribed and over-the-counter medication under strict guidelines. Some schools choose not to undertake the responsibility.

Preschools that do administer medication require, by law, a written request from the parent and sometimes an ad-

ditional form from the pediatrician. All medications must be in their original containers and clearly labeled with the child's name, the name of the medication, the dosage, and the physician's name. Your child's school may have additional requirements for administering medication.

Transportation and
School Attendance

Who should bring my child to and from school?

Most children, at least for the first few sessions of school, want their parent to bring them and pick them up, but this is often not practical when both parents work. Many children these days are brought to school and picked up by a nanny or grandparent. This arrangement works well if it is the same person each time who is doing the dropping off and picking up.

Experience shows that *how* the children are dropped off and picked up is more important than the *who*. Cheerful words can make all the difference: "Have a wonderful morning! I'll be back to pick you up, and then we can go home and make lunch together" (or whatever activity is next on the agenda). As long as the person is warm, affectionate, and genuinely caring, the child is happy.

Being punctual is essential at dismissal time. It is much better for the adult to be a few minutes early for pickup and wait for the child than it is for the child to see everyone else leave while he waits to be picked up. How wonderful it is for a child to run into welcoming arms at the end of a busy morning at school!

What if I'm late picking my child up from school?

Sometimes being late is unavoidable. If you know that you are going to be late picking up your child, call the school office and let them know. If you are in your car with no telephone, feeling panicked about being late, *don't speed!* There is no need to panic. If your child is the last one left in the classroom or outside, take comfort in the fact that the teacher will reassure your child that you are indeed on your way. Someone will stay with him until you arrive.

Of course, apologies are in order to the person who has had to stay late to care for your child, and hugs and apologies are owed to your child. No harm done—once or twice. Schools frown heavily on parents who are habitually late. Some schools charge for every minute past dismissal time. Ask your school about its policy.

It usually takes only one late arrival and the sight of your precious little one with quivering chin asking where you were to make any parent resolve never to be late again.

Are car pools a good idea?

When families live in the same neighborhood, it is sometimes advantageous to form car pools, whereby one parent agrees to drive children to school and another parent agrees to bring the children home from school. Another arrangement is to schedule driving on specific days of the week.

Unless parents are working full-time and have no choice, car pooling to and from preschool preferably should not begin until the little ones have surmounted the "school separation anxiety" period. Once the children are well settled in, there should be no problem if:

★ All cars are well maintained and safe.

★ You always know who is driving.

★ You trust the drivers.

★ Your child likes the drivers and their children.

★ All car seats conform to safety regulations.

★ Plans are made ahead of time in the event no one is home to receive a child.

★ Car pooling is a pleasant experience for your child.

It is a good idea to ride along with your child the first time she is picked up by another parent. You can then evaluate the demeanor and driving skills of the driver and share this first experience with your child. Sometimes schools are able to provide parents lists of families in their zip code who are interested in car pooling.

Should I take my child out of school for family trips?

Yes! I tell parents that this is not college. Their child will not be missing midterms or finals. Family time should be a priority. Imagine the child's excitement upon returning to school. There is so much to tell about the airplane or train ride to Grandma's, or Disney World, or visiting out-of-town cousins.

I also suggest that if the family has returned home very late at night from the trip, they not awaken the child the next day for school. The child can use the extra sleep, and one day of reorienting to being home before returning to school is always a good idea.

Will it harm my child if we move during the school year?

The center of a child's universe, after himself, is his family. His happiness, security, and well-being are dependent on the family. If the family needs to move during the school year, the child will certainly miss his friends, his teachers, and especially his routine. But as long as a child is with his family, he trusts that he will be all right. What is most important to the child who is going to move is preparation. The teacher can be of great help in this area.

Tell your child's teacher the date of the move and what your child has been told. When you and the teacher think it is appropriate, you may ask your child if he would like to tell his school friends about his "special moving news." The teacher may then take the opportunity to open a discussion, perhaps at circle time, about what it means to move and all the feelings the family who is moving may have. There are also children's books about moving that may be read at home and shared at school.

A vital part of the preparation is to assure and reassure your child that all members of the family will be moving and will be together (thereby taking care of those developmental issues of abandonment) and that his toys will be coming, his crib or bed, his clothing, his pets, and anything else that you know is important to him. Ask that the teacher reiterate in class whatever you have told your child. Undoubtedly, the teacher will have the other children make some sort of re-membrance gift for your child. After the move, be sure to help your child make a picture, write a letter, or send a photo of the new house to his former classmates. A move, even in the middle of the school year, can be a valuable learning ex-perience not only for your child but for all the children in the class.

Whenever a child is going to move away from the area or even to a different part of town, we bring our dollhouse to the middle of the circle and play "moving." We drive one of the class trucks up to the dollhouse and let the child who is moving be the Mover. The Mover gets to take all the furniture out of the dollhouse and load it onto the moving truck. A big production is made about the fact that the entire family is going also (even the new baby that the child may have am-bivalent feelings about). This is a good time for a teacher to

really listen to detect feelings of sadness or fright. That information should certainly be shared with the parents.

We take a class photo, have it framed, and present it to the child on his last day, along with paintings and drawings from the children. Then we all participate in a last group hug. Usually for months after a child's departure, when I ask who is not in our morning circle that day, several children will invariably say the name of the child who has moved away. Preparation and closure are important not only to the child who is moving but to the friends left behind as well.

"What If
My Child . . . ?"

What if my child hits or bites?

Very young children do not yet have a well-developed sense of cause-and-effect relationships. They hit or bite because they are feeling frustrated, and hitting or biting is a quick release. At that moment they may not even be aware that hitting or biting hurts. They know they are feeling angry or frustrated and do not yet have all the verbal skills necessary to express their feelings. Hitting or biting is simply a nonverbal expression of anger.

When the child is old enough and capable of using the word *no*, incidents of biting decrease markedly—usually by the age of three. When there is a child who bites in a school situation, the staff will be extremely vigilant. These children are closely watched and supervised so that incidents are prevented before they occur. When bites do occur, the teacher should react quickly by telling the biter, "No biting!" The child who was bitten will be given the necessary attention and consoled, and the bitten area will be washed. The child who did the biting will then be talked to and given time to calm down. Both set of parents will be notified.

"Use your words" is a popular phrase among teachers. Children often need to be reminded that they should communicate verbally and that they don't need to hit, whine, or bite in frustration. Younger or less mature children have low impulse control, so until they master the verbal skills to ask for what they want, they will be closely watched by the adults around them.

The teacher needs to be notified if your child has, in the past, had a tendency to bite. It may not happen in school, but the teacher needs to know so the adults in class can be nearby to help your child find other ways to express anger and frustration.

What if my child won't/can't sit still?

Most children come into the preschool situation not knowing very much about what is expected of them. They know they will be painting and playing with toys. So far, so good.

Ample time is allowed for "free play" in the first year of preschool. The young child is encouraged to move around the classroom, touching, exploring, and investigating. The teacher may at some point call all the children together to sit in a group and sing songs, listen to a book, discuss the weather, or play a group game. Most children come running. Some, at the beginning of the school year, do not. Some children are simply not interested in sitting and will continue to walk around while keeping an eye on the proceedings. There is no point in trying to coerce a uninterested child into joining a structured activity. Early childhood educators recognize the need for children to move. It's difficult for some little ones to sit and attend for more than a minute or two at the beginning of the year. If the activity is interesting and

exciting enough, even the most reluctant wanderer will join the group.

If by the middle of the school year a child seems unable to sit and pay attention, it's probably time for a parent–teacher conference. The teacher needs to know what the child is doing at home, and she needs to let the parents know (if they haven't already been told) that the child seems unable to sit and attend for very long. Many young children are by nature "movers." They are busy little people with no time to sit. As they mature and their attention span grows, they will join the group. Occasionally, a child will have a very real attention-span problem. Allowances will be made for the child who simply cannot sit and pay attention in class. The teacher may then suggest that the parents consult with their child's pediatrician or arrange for a consultation by a developmental specialist.

What if my child sucks her thumb?

For some children, the thumb is a comfort item that can never be taken away. It's always there when needed. It's always there when wanted. So we have to make the distinction between needed and wanted. Especially in school.

Has your child fallen and hurt herself? Yes, the thumb is probably needed, even when the teacher is administering comfort and hugs. Is your child wandering around the classroom unfocused, sucking her thumb? The thumb in that case is probably just wanted. Wanted, for lack of something

better to do. It's the teacher's job at that point to swoop in and get your child involved in something interesting.

We see thumb sucking in preschool when children are frightened, hurt, tired, or bored. We comfort the frightened and hurt, we make sure the parents are alerted to the tired, and we take responsibility for the bored. We are there to provide the guidance that will help children select something interesting to do. A child may be encouraged to try a new puzzle or art material or become involved in a pretend play situation. During story time it is common to see the resumption of thumb sucking when the child is relaxed.

Occasional thumb sucking by young children in the classroom is not seen as a problem. If a teacher believes that it is excessive and indicative of other problems, the parents will be notified. If you are concerned, discuss it with the teacher.

What if my child needs a blanket, pacifier, bottle, or other transitional object?

Some children are better able to separate if a transitional object (Blankie or Doggy) is brought to school with them. Early childhood teachers should understand the child's need to see and touch a comfort item that smells like, looks like, and reminds them of home. Holding their cherished item for the first few days of school provides the comfort and reassurance needed to successfully separate. The teacher will then prob-

ably suggest that the item be placed in the child's cubby (in full view, of course) while the child plays. That enables the child to visit and touch this beloved item whenever he may need a comfort "fix."

Pacifiers and bottles are a different story. Symbolically, these are baby items and school is for "big kids," but many children of preschool age still need their pacifier or bottle. If a child walks around in class with a pacifier, he is certainly physically inhibited from talking. At times, the child may be so involved with his pacifier that it prevents him from participating fully in the program. The main concern with having a bottle or pacifier in the classroom is the probability of other children handling these items. This, of course, would be a very real health concern. Therefore the use of these objects in school is discouraged.

Many parents begin talking to their child about curtailing the public usage of these items the summer before school begins. Most children accept the limitation of using the bottle and pacifier only at home or in the car or wherever else the parent feels is appropriate. These items can be waiting for your child in the car at the end of the school morning. If your child seems dependent on one of these oral comfort items, talk to the teacher and see what she would suggest about weaning your child away at least during school hours. As the child grows more confident and independent, the need for these transitional objects decreases.

What if my child takes things from school?

It is not uncommon for young children to bring home things that do not belong to them. When classroom toys are brought home without permission, the parents are usually the only ones who are concerned.

When this happens in my class, I tell the parents that I consider it flattering. I believe that the child who has taken a toy is transferring to home the good feelings he has about school. He has taken some of school home with him. That's fine.

What is not fine is taking something without permission. So when the parent returns the object the next day, I meet with the child and parent for a few minutes after school and we talk about it. I usually say, "The Bunny Book went home with you yesterday and I didn't know where it was. I'm glad you brought it back. Would you like to *borrow* it until tomorrow?"

We talk about what borrowing means and what returning means. The child is always happy (and relieved) to borrow something from the class. We usually part with my reinforcing the concept by saying, "I'm glad you are borrowing a book you like. I will be happy when it's returned so everyone can enjoy it."

The child has learned a valuable lesson with his dignity intact. This technique works equally well for parents at home.

In my experience, children learn more from gentle instruction than from guilt-producing accusations.

What if my child is left-handed?

Gone are the days when stern, topknotted teachers brought rulers down on tiny left hands holding crayons. These days we know that handedness is genetically determined and best left unchallenged and unchanged. Handedness is generally not determined until the age of three or even beyond. Most children often alternate hands for the first few years of life. Children under the age of three who predominantly use the left hand are often mistakenly labeled "lefties."

In preschool, when a child is observed using the left hand consistently for painting, drawing, reaching, and eating, the teacher will place the brushes, crayons, and crackers in front of the child at the midline (in line with the middle of the chest) and continue to observe which hand is used for grabbing. Left-handed scissors are available for children who seem more comfortable using them. There are also universal scissors available that may be used with either hand. In school, children who switch objects from the right hand to the left will not be asked to use only the right hand.

If you believe your child to be left-handed, alert the teachers so that they can observe your child at school and make accommodations when necessary. Wait and see before labeling a child left-handed.

What if my child doesn't talk yet?

Talking is not a requirement for preschool. Two-year-old children who are not developmentally ready to use expressive language (talking) can and do experience all the rich benefits of preschool. Most children are skilled at finding ways to make their needs known. Nonverbal children have as much fun exploring and playing as their more verbal playmates.

Some awkward moments may occur, perhaps, during a circle time when other children are responding in kind to a cheery "Good morning." A sensitive teacher might simply wave to the nonverbal child while saying "Good morning" and ask the child to wave back. The child is then participating in a satisfying way and feels more part of the group.

Parents should always confer with the teacher so that everyone is working together on mutually agreed-upon strategies for facilitating language. Some children are selectively mute in school for a period of time, usually at the beginning of the school year. No pressure should be put on the children who cannot or choose not to talk while in school. The teacher can make the nonverbal child feel included by saying such things as, "I can see by your eyes that you know the answer." Parents can say that at home, too.

The children who are not yet talking in school are invariably taking in all of the experiences around them. At

music time, they may sit and watch and later sing at home, or they may begin to sing the songs they learned months before.

If the parent or the teacher has a real concern about the lack or clarity of expressive language, a conference should be held and an evaluation with a speech pathologist scheduled. The most common phrase we hear from the speech pathologist is "It's an age-appropriate language delay. Give the child tincture of time."

Each September, I have in my class at least one child who will not talk aloud in a group. It certainly is understandable, and I liken it to stage fright. When it is that particular child's turn to say "Good morning" in the circle, and all eyes are upon her, speaking aloud is too frightening. I usually say, "You're saying good morning inside your mouth, aren't you? That's okay, maybe next time you will let it out." I believe that we need to have enough respect for children to allow them time to work through their shyness themselves. After a period of time, if no progress is made in the classroom, I will speak to the parents who are, more often than not, shocked to hear that their child has not been talking at all in school. "She is a chatterbox at home! She relates the entire morning's happenings. We even heard that you had a Band-Aid on your finger last week," they exclaim. I tell the parents that I see this every year and that it is not a big concern.

If the parents choose, they may make a lighthearted game at home by playing "circle time." The parents ask, "Who will be Doris?" Usually the child will insist upon this role (control). The parents can be the children and talk about the weather or news or an upcoming holiday, or sing a

song. The child should be allowed to control the circle. This creates an atmosphere of comfort about speaking in a group which will eventually transfer to school. When parents announce in front of their child that "Susan is shy," I say brightly, "Susan is just *feeling* shy right now." I gently counsel parents not to label their child. Shyness may be fleeting— labels are not.

What if my child refuses to do any artwork?

At dismissal time, you see all the other children excitedly showing their art project to whoever is picking them up. You hear appreciative oohs and ahhs around the classroom. Your child's tote bag is empty. Does that mean he did nothing that morning? On the contrary.

Some children are far too busy to come and sit at the table to do an art project. They much prefer to engage in imaginative play with a friend (for example, firefighters or preparing a meal in the house corner), or block building, sand or water play, woodworking, Play-Doh, puzzles, puppets, or any number of wonderful activities that stimulate the senses, develop social skills, encourage language development, and foster creativity. None of these wonderful experiences can be placed in a tote bag for you to see.

The teacher will certainly continue to encourage your child to try some arts-and-crafts activities, while recognizing that some children do have a stronger interest in other areas. Sooner or later, every child will experiment with art materials. It's guaranteed that during the school year you will have at least a few pieces of artwork to display.

When a child is only interested in building with blocks or playing with cars and trucks day after day and cannot be coaxed to the art table, I try to make the prospect of doing artwork as irresistible as possible. I sometimes say, "Michael, bring one of those cars over here to this tray of paint. Let's drive the car through it and see what the tire tracks look like on this big piece of paper." Voilà—tire art! If a child is stuck at the sandbox, I might invite her to bring some sand to the art table, offer some glue to drizzle on paper, drop some sand on it, and see what happens—sand art! Everything can be turned into art with a little imagination. Children learn that materials can and should be used many ways and that art is not just painting and drawing but experimentation and fun.

What if my child refuses to eat the snack at school?

There are many possible reasons a child does not eat at snack time in school. At the beginning of the school year, snack time may present yet another set of bewildering rules and behaviors to learn. The children may be expected to wait until everyone is seated. They may be expected to wait until a blessing is recited. It is a rude awakening to some that requests for certain foods are not honored as they are at home.

Because no child is forced to eat in school, the power struggles parents sometimes endure at home do not occur in the classroom. Teachers, for the most part, can have a cava-

lier attitude about whether or not the children eat their snack, because they know that no child will perish from hunger before going home for lunch. Experience shows that when a new food is served, there are always voracious eaters who set an example by enthusiastically finishing everything set before them. Even the most timid eaters tend to at least try a few bites in the presence of such peer pressure.

In some schools, parents are invited to bring in or prepare snack with the class. Even if your school does not have this policy, parents of timid eaters certainly may ask to send in their own child's favorite nutritious snack to share with the class. Snack time at school should be a social, relaxed, and enjoyable part of the day. The child who chooses not to eat is nevertheless enjoying table talk and the camaraderie of his peers without feeling pressure to eat.

What if my child spills?

Spilling is part of the job description for two- and three-year-olds. Developmentally, those little fingers think they can do more than they actually can. The important thing is that the children are trying. They are trying to handle containers of sand, cups of milk, containers of blocks, puzzles, beads—anything that holds something else. They are gaining mastery of this important skill, which encompasses hand-eye coordination, spatial relations, and all types of other developmental goodies.

Teachers expect spills. Lots of them. This is one of the

reasons for asking for an extra set of clothing to be kept in the classroom.

On the very first school day in my class, I spill my cup of milk on the snack table. As twelve pair of eyes scan my face expectantly, I say simply, "Oh, I spilled. That's okay. Everyone spills sometime. I'll just clean it up." The collective sigh of relief is audible.

What if my child won't participate during group activities?

Some children may need to ease rather than jump into situations. That is their M.O. (modus operandi). We must respect their decision to watch rather than participate at that particular moment in time. There is always a toy or activity that will look tempting enough to try. For example: "Jamie, these farm animals might run away. Will you please bring me two of those big blocks over there, and we can build a fence for the animals. Oh-oh, two blocks are not enough. What shall we do? Good idea! Bring more blocks. Amy, will you help your friend Jamie bring some blocks for the animal fence?"

The teacher can then ease herself out of the play situation when Jamie is involved in play with another child. Or in the kitchen area, the teacher could sit at the small table and say, "Jamie, I am so hungry. I wish someone would cook some breakfast for me. Here is my plate. Will you please put some food on it for me? Thank you. Shall we call some friends over? I bet they are hungry too." Once Jamie is involved with other children, the teacher can then ease out of that play sit-

uation. Some children need the teacher to facilitate a play scenario for them until they feel more comfortable doing it themselves in a group.

Preschoolers devote lots of energy to experimenting and discovering what things they like to do. Some children need longer observation times before deciding to join in an activity. This occurs mainly at the beginning of the morning.

Be assured that the teacher will try to entice your reticent child into some sort of play. Early childhood educators know how to be encouraging without forcing. There is always a toy or activity that will look tempting enough to try.

Because two-year-olds enjoy repetition and sameness, they easily fall into patterns and habits. Some children enjoy the attention they receive when they don't participate. But eventually, just standing around becomes boring and the child will move toward an activity without prompting from the teacher.

We help children by respecting their individual styles of approaching play situations. If the teacher feels the withdrawal behavior is going on much too long and has become a problem, she will let you know. You can then discuss strategies for helping your child change these patterns.

What if my child prefers free play to a specific activity?

Every program provides lots of free play time. It's important for every child to be able to learn to make choices. Choosing to play in the sandbox instead of painting at the easel en-

ables a child to feel good about his newfound autonomy. Free play is so named because it allows the child the freedom of making those kinds of choices. He can make a new choice every two minutes if he wants to. He can play alone, or he can play with one friend. He can join a group or just watch. What power!

When the teacher calls everyone for circle time, or music class, or creative movement, or science for some structured time, the child's choices are to come running with everyone else or to continue playing. The child who continues playing while everyone else is sitting and attending will no doubt receive a personal invitation from the teacher. No child should ever be forced to join an activity. If the teacher makes the structured activity look like enough fun, any child will be enticed to join the group. At the very beginning of the school year, some children may need time to play on the periphery of a structured activity. While they play quietly, they are watching the activity and learning what to expect. They are taking part and enjoying themselves vicariously. More often than not, they will join in next time.

Taking part in classroom structured activities is developmental. Toddlers are expected to have a difficult time settling down and attending to any one activity for more than a few minutes. If a four-year-old cannot or will not join the rest of the class in any structured activity, that may be considered problematic behavior. Parents and teachers will need to work together to determine whether outside help is warranted.

What if my daughter plays only with girls, or my son only with boys?

No matter how hard we try to make toys and games gender-neutral, and try not to orchestrate gender differences by our attitudes, toys will generally be used differently by girls and by boys. In any preschool classroom, one finds dolls, blocks, a kitchen area, cars and trucks, perhaps a workbench, and many gender-neutral toys and activities. Over the course of twenty-five years, I have observed the same roles played out year after year. Generally speaking, most girls play with the dolls in a nurturing role, and most boys play with cars and trucks or build with blocks. If a boy plays with a doll in a carriage, he is likely to be racing with the carriage, unmindful of its inhabitant. If a girl builds with blocks, it is usually not a tall tower to be knocked down with glee, but perhaps a castle for a princess, or a place for animals to play. Even though gunplay is forbidden in most classrooms, boys will use a block, a cardboard tube, or a finger to shoot with. It just doesn't seem to occur to girls that shooting might be a fun thing to do.

There are ages and stages of development where boys hate girls and girls hate boys, and they will be friends only with kids of the same gender. That happens in elementary school. In preschool, if girls are playing only with girls, and

boys are playing only with boys, it is because they are united through common activities.

Two girls in my class donned tutus and danced gracefully with scarves after seeing a ballet performance in school. When the boys asked for scarves, I was delighted, thinking they were responding to the melodic strains of the "Waltz of the Flowers." Within seconds, while the girls twirled, the boys were swatting each other with the scarves. Need I say more?

What if my child is being bullied?

For three days in a row, your child tells you that Bobby hits him when they are on the playground. Now your child doesn't want to go to school, let alone the playground. This calls for immediate action. Call the teacher at home, explain what your child has related to you, and ask if she has time to speak with you about the problem.

If the teacher says she is aware of the problem and that all of the playground staff are watching Bobby closely now, you should ask why you weren't informed of the problem earlier. Or, if Bobby's M.O. was to hit and run when no one was watching, and your child didn't cry or tell a teacher, this information may come as a surprise to the teacher. If that is the case, your child needs some help with knowing how and when to communicate his needs to the teacher. Tell the teacher that you will work with your child at home by teaching him assertiveness skills ("Don't hit me. I don't like it! I'm telling the teacher").

Ask for assurance that Bobby will similarly be helped. It goes without saying that Bobby clearly needs help in curbing his unacceptable behavior. Also, ask if the teacher would be willing to talk to the class, in general terms, about friendship, feelings, and appropriate conduct at school. I would play a problem-solving game with the class, throwing out such questions as: "What would you do if someone hit you at school? Why would someone hit a friend? Is it nice to hit?" (The hitter needs to hear that the entire class thinks that hitting is not nice.) "What could you do instead of hitting if you were feeling angry?" Peer pressure works. Every child wants to be accepted. It is helpful to the bully and his victims to learn acceptable behaviors from their peers as well as from their parents and teachers.

If all else fails, invite Bobby and his mom to your home for a play date. The best thing that could happen is that your child and Bobby will become friends.

What if my child refuses to get dressed?

Part of the early-morning routine is getting dressed. Your youngster refuses to get dressed when you are in the midst of a hectic morning. What do you do? The first time it happens and you are caught by surprise with fifteen minutes to get out of the house, there are not many options. The most expedient solution is to give the old "It's your choice. Will you put it on yourself, or shall I help you? Choose now." That evening have your child pick out what she wants to wear to

school the next day. She may need your help. You can show her two different shirts and ask, "Do you want to choose the red one or the blue one?" Accept her choices and ask her where the clothing should be placed so she can find them the next morning. You can ask if she wants some help getting dressed.

If this solution stops working after a while, you can always go back to the expedient solution. Being given those types of choices is empowering to your child. It builds self-esteem while setting limits.

One day a mother came into my classroom carrying her two-and-a-half-year-old son, who was wearing a smile and a diaper and nothing else. She put him down and he immediately ran to the sand table. The mother explained that Alex had refused to dress, so she brought him to school with his clothing in a plastic bag. I simply said to him, "Alex, I see that you are ready to play, but in school you need to be dressed. Do you want Mommy to dress you, or shall I?"

"Mommy," he quickly replied. Alex allowed himself to be dressed in a flash and went off to play again. He was given an appropriate choice, and morning stress was completely avoided. What a mom!

What if my child wants to pick out her own clothes?

Part of the joy of gaining independence is the satisfaction that comes with making choices. Very young children have precious little choice in their daily lives. They are told when to go, where to go, how to go.

If your child wants to select his own clothing for school, let him. If the colors or patterns don't coordinate, so what? The pride and satisfaction he feels in having been allowed to make these choices are what's important. We have seen many a frazzled parent come to school (with a teary-eyed child in tow) after a morning battle over choice of clothing. How can a child be expected to have a fun morning after a power struggle over something so inconsequential?

Parents who allow their children to make their own choices may come in announcing, "Danny chose his own out-fit today." The teacher may comment on how colorful everything looks, and Danny goes off to play feeling proud and happy. If you feel embarrassed that your child is wearing a favorite pajama top, striped shorts, and cowboy boots, remember that it is you who is embarrassed, not your child. The teachers will be amused, and the other children will probably not notice. What will the other parents think? They will think that you are secure enough to allow your child to be creative and independent. You will be admired.

What if my child won't eat breakfast before school?

Mealtimes are an important ritual in some households, but weekday breakfasts may not be the best time to enforce these routines. Some children simply cannot eat breakfast in a rush. If your child, for whatever reason, won't or can't eat on those hectic early mornings, keep your cool and get creative. The cool part: "Oh, you don't want to eat? That's okay." The creative part: "Would you rather eat now or take a picnic in the car today?" Toast, bagels, and small boxes of dry cereal travel well. It's just not worth the aggravation of an early-morning power struggle. Breakfast should be a routine and pleasurable experience.

If despite your best efforts, no food has passed your child's lips, tell the teacher. She can either slip him a cracker or allow him to nibble from the "picnic" in his tote bag. In any case, snack time is only a couple of hours away. That morning the teacher may take the opportunity to talk with the class about the value of eating breakfast. Somehow because the teacher says it, breakfast becomes more important.

What if my child suddenly refuses to go to school?

Your child has settled into the routine of school and is having a positive experience. Unexpectedly, one morning he refuses to go to school. He seems clearly unhappy at the prospect and can't or won't say why. You cajole him into going to school and the teacher tells you that he seems fine and that he has not observed any indication of unhappiness. Yet, the next few school mornings bring repeat performances of a tearful "I don't want to go."

It is time to play detective. Schedule a conference with the teacher. Ask yourself what changes have occurred at home recently. Is anyone sick? Is anyone traveling? Have new demands been made on your child? (For example, goodbye crib, hello big bed; goodbye bottle or pacifier; goodbye diapers.)

Is anyone visiting? And finally, have there been changes in the sleep pattern of your child or changes in behavior at home?

When you meet with the teacher, ask for an overview of your child's day at school. Ask if there have been any changes. Has your child cried at school? If so, why, and what was done about it? Your detective work will probably pay off. After you have gathered information and shared yours, you and the teacher very well may come up with some likely possibilities for your child's early morning unhappiness. Once you have detected a possible problem, you and the teacher can work on a solution that will bring the sparkle back to your child's eyes on a school morning.

In my experience, when this happens with children under the age of three and a half, it is usually related to toilet training. Occasionally, pressure is brought to bear by well-meaning parents who think it is time for their child to be in underpants. Many times the child feels conflicted. His head tells him that he is a big boy, and he certainly wants to please his parents, but his bladder is not cooperating. At home, when the toilet is nearby and Mom is there reminding him, things go pretty well. At school, when there are so many fun things to do and friends to play with, accidents will happen. No matter how kindly and gently the teacher treats the accident, some children feel guilt. He may feel that it is better to stay home and feel safe. He certainly can't tell Mom the reason. Sometimes a child isn't even aware of the reason for not wanting to go to school.

In these instances, I suggest that the parents ask the child what he would like to wear to school, giving him the choice of diapers, pull-up training pants, or underwear. If he

says "diapers," then diapers it is, for now. The parents can tell him that he can try again when he is feeling a bit bigger. The child returns to school happy and relaxed.

What if my child has difficulty separating from the teacher at the end of the year?

The separation unit at the end of the school year is every bit as important as the separation unit at the beginning of the school year. At the beginning, the child had to learn to say goodbye to Mom and Dad and learn to function as an individual, apart from them.

The same sense of separation can occur for the child at the close of the school year. The teacher has earned the trust and affection of the children. The children think of themselves as part of a special group; they have bonded. The concept of themselves away from their beloved teacher and away from their group does not occur to them until the end of the school year.

I start using a large calendar at the beginning of the school year. We sing songs about the names of the days of the week, and we talk about holidays that occur each month. The children's names are printed on each day, so we know who the weather person will be that morning. And most important, we notice that there are X's on the days we do not come to school.

I explain that when the children see an X on the calen-

dar (other than Saturday or Sunday) that is a day that they stay home and play with their own toys, go on a trip, or visit someone. There is no school on an X day. When December comes and the children notice a series of X's in a row, we talk about winter break.

After May, when I turn the calendar page and we see that June has only a few days of school, and the rest of the page is filled with X's, the children's eyes open wide. What can this mean? July and August are Xed, also. I explain that all these X's mean that there is a long vacation at the end of this school year. The last day of school is marked with a sad face and a happy face symbol. We talk about having sad and happy feelings at the same time—sad because it's the end of the school year, and happy because they have grown in so many wonderful ways.

I reminisce about the beginning of school: "Remember when you first came to school and most of you cried? Why did you cry?" They answer that they wanted their mommy or daddy or that they felt scared. I ask if they still cry when they come to school. As one, they all shout, "No!" I ask why. They answer, "We're big now!" I seize the opportunity and continue. "Right. You are so big now that after the long summer vacation, you get to go to a Big Kid class!" (Said with much excitement.) Then we take a tour of the Big Kid classes and we see that not only are there fabulous toys, but there are easels, blocks, books, and many other familiar playthings that they love. And best of all, most of the Big Kid rooms have animals or fish (neither of which I have). Then we come back to our own room and talk about what we saw and the names of the teachers and the rooms.

The next school day, we look at the calendar again, and we review what all the X's mean. I again tell them that they are so big that they get to go to the Big Kid classes after the summer and that little tiny kids will come crying into our classroom. There is usually a minute or two of silence while they consider this information.

I continue, "But I will always be here to give you a hug, because you will always be special to me and I love you. So you can stop by the classroom before you go to your Big Kids class next year and I will have a hug for you—always."

I bring a big empty carton into the room and explain that all the toys need to be washed and packed away for the summer. All the children are encouraged to wash or dry some toys and place them in the carton. This is a very important, concrete act of closure. The children actually take part in the closing of our classroom in a way that is both symbolic and real to them.

On the last day of school, we have a favorite-food party, to which the parents are invited. Before the final snack, I hold up the calendar and ask the children to explain the sad and happy face symbols to their parents and to also explain what all the X's mean. We then have our final party snack, go to the playground, and say goodbye. In all, this final separation unit is a seemingly casual but very important experience for the children. They leave feeling very big and proud, secure in the knowledge that they can always come back for a hug. And they do!

How to Help Your Child to Separate from the Teacher at the End of the School Year

★ Help your child make a special goodbye picture or card for the teacher. Ask your child how she can show her feelings for the teacher in the picture. Will it be a rainbow, a happy or sad face, perhaps a picture of your child with the teacher? Let the idea come from your child and let her do it by herself. The teacher will love it.

★ Have your child take a photograph of his teacher with an inexpensive camera and suggest that the teacher wave goodbye in the photo. Or take one of your child and the teacher together.

★ Ask the teacher if your child may call her during the summer. If the teacher says yes, tell your child that he will be able to talk to the teacher even after school is over.

★ Have your child keep in touch with the children in his class over the summer. Find out which ones will be in his class next year and suggest play dates with them.

Afterword

The Transition from Preschool to Kindergarten

Leaving preschool can be an emotionally wrenching experience for some parents. So before you can help your child leave the nurturing environment of preschool, you need to address your own ambivalent feelings. In all likelihood, you will never again have the freedom to peek in and watch your child whenever you want to. You probably won't see or speak to her teacher as often as you did in preschool. Along with the pride and delight you feel at your child's growth, you may feel a vague sense of mourning for the loss of this wonderful part of your child's life experience. These feelings are not unlike the ones you felt before she began preschool. It is the beginning of a new journey for your child and for you.

Once you, your child's preschool teacher, and her pediatrician agree that she is indeed ready for kindergarten (some children do need one more year of preschool), it's time once again to assess your options for schools. After you establish whether your child will be attending her neighborhood public school or a private school, set about preparing her for the transition from preschool to her new school.

In the spring, before the preschool year is over, be sure your child knows the name of her elementary school and has at least seen the building and grounds. Both you and your child will want to familiarize yourselves with the new school.

Most schools have an orientation program for all incoming kindergarten children. Plan to attend with your child. If your neighborhood school does not offer an orientation program, schedule a visit to the school anyway. Elementary schools are much more formal than preschools, so the freedom to explore is limited. Find out which other children from your child's preschool will be attending the new school and try and help your child establish those friendships. Perhaps you and another parent can make an appointment to show your future kindergartners the school and kindergarten classrooms together. If you are visiting during school hours, watch your child for signs of anxiety about the large size of the school, the large size of some of the children, and the large numbers of children. (Notice the pattern?) The new school is BIG. Your child may see all of this as exciting. But if it seems more frightening to her than exciting, have a little talk when you get home. Talk about how she felt before she started preschool. Point out that it is natural to have all the same feelings again. Remind her of how much she enjoys preschool now and assure her that she will feel the same about her new school.

Ask her teacher what special activities are planned for the end of the school year. Closure is very important, especially this year. Making too big a deal about leaving preschool and going to kindergarten, however, is counterproductive. The teacher is sure to tell the children that they will be welcomed anytime they can come back for a visit. Some schools have a little graduation ceremony for the children who are leaving, and others feel that even this is too much. A wise teacher won't issue stern and scary warnings about how

different kindergarten might be from preschool. The children don't need to be alarmed by images of having to sit at desks for long periods of time, or expectations of having to be proficient at reading and writing. It is unrealistic and unnecessary to describe what they might expect from their new school. They should end their preschool years secure in the knowledge that their teachers and parents believe them to be capable, wonderful, and ready for kindergarten.

It has been a magical journey. Now your child is setting off on another exciting adventure.

The First Day of Kindergarten

I wish my mom could stay with me
for just a little while, I'd plea.
It's scary here among this crowd.
If only my mom were allowed
to be with me, to hold my hand.
She'd smile at me, she'd understand.
She'd know I'm feeling scared and small.
She'd prob'ly wink and say, "Stand tall."
I'd listen to those words and try
to lift my head up, way up high.
But will they like me, give respect,
pay attention, or reject?
Here come the kids, they're running in.
I'll try my best to fake a grin,
but deep inside I want my mommy.
Oh, how I wish that I could reach her.
I hope these kids do not suspect
how hard it is to be the teacher.

DORIS HERMAN

Appendix

Recommended Resources for Parents

BOOKS

Today's parents have a wide range of classic child development books to choose from, such as those by T. Berry Brazelton and Penelope Leach, and the reliable Dr. Benjamin Spock's *Baby and Child Care*. My favorite reference on child development is the Gesell Institute's *Child Behavior: The Classic Child Care Manual*. It is a nonjudgmental guide about each stage of children's development. Some other worthwhile books about child development are:

Miseducation, by David Elkind (Knopf, 1988).

How to Talk So Kids Will Listen and Listen So Kids Will Talk, by Adele Faber and Elaine Mazlish (Avon, 1991).

What to Expect in the Toddler Years, by Arlene Eisenberg, Heidi E. Murkoff, and Sandee E. Hathaway (Workman, 1994).

Who's in Control? by Lawrence Balter (Poseidon Press, 1988, out of print).

The Preschool Years, by Ellen Galinsky and Judy David (Ballantine, 1991).

Raising Preschoolers, by Sylvia Rimm (Random House, 1997).

The Magic Years, by Selma H. Fraiberg (Fireside, 1996).

Toddlers and Preschoolers, by Lawrence Kutner (Avon, 1995).

It's often helpful to read storybooks to your children to help them make the transition to preschool and kindergarten. I recommend the following books geared for children entering preschool, particularly during the summer before preschool (those listed as "out of print" can be found at the library but not the bookstore):

First Day of School, by Helen Oxenbury (Puffin, 1993).

Kathryn Goes to Nursery School, by Jill Krementz (Random House, 1986, out of print).

Chatterbox Jamie, by Nancy Evans Cooney (Putnam, 1993, out of print).

Will I Have a Friend? by Miriam Cohen (Alladin, 1989).

My Nursery School, by Harlow Rockwell (Mulberry Books, 1990; first published 1967).

Shawn Goes to School, by Petronella Breinburg (Harpercrest, 1974).

Monster Goes to School, by Virginia Mueller (Albert Whitman, 1997).

The Berenstain Bears Go to School, by Stan and Jan Berenstain (Random House, 1978).

Children in their last year of preschool will enjoy these books to help them prepare for kindergarten:

My First Days of School, by Jane Hamilton-Merrit (Julian Messner, 1982, out of print).

School Days, by B. G. Hennessy (Demco Media, 1992).

When You Go to Kindergarten, by James Howe (Mulberry Books, 1995).

Alice Ann Gets Ready for School, by Cynthia Jabar (Joyst Books, 1989, out of print).

When Will I Read? by Miriam Cohen (Bantam Doubleday Dell, 1996).

MAGAZINES

Several magazines have regular parenting and educational columns and features relating to preschools and preschool-age children. Here is a listing of some of the more popular family magazines that might be of interest to parents of young children:

Parents. Specific to women with growing children. Features articles on age-specific child development, education, and discipline. To order: (800) 727-3682.

Parenting. Articles about health, education, and discipline. To order: (800) 234-0847.

Child. Specific to first-time parents. Information on education, behavior, play, health, and nutrition. To order: (800) 777-0222.

Family Life. A magazine for parents of children aged three to twelve. To order: (212) 767-6000.

THE INTERNET

The World Wide Web has become a useful source of information on two fronts: listings of preschool options in your area, and chat rooms where parents of preschoolers can exchange ideas and experiences. New parent support groups

appear regularly, and every year more and more preschools become Internet-savvy and create their own Web site.

Care Guide
http://www.careguide.net

Nationwide listings of preschools, day-care, and elder-care programs.

Parent Soup
http://parentsoup.com

Parents Place
http://parentsplace.com

Two comprehensive parenting sites on iVillage.com, The Women's Network, for parents of children in every age group from infants to teenagers. Includes articles, bulletin boards, and chat rooms.

Parents Helping Parents
http://www.php.com

A wonderful resource for parents of children with special needs, with categories including chat rooms, support groups, a resource directory, calendars of events throughout the country, new technologies for children with special needs, health insurance information, safety issues, and a bookstore.

ORGANIZATIONS

National Association for the Education of Young Children (NAEYC)

A wonderful organization, to which I refer throughout this book. In addition to accrediting preschools, the NAEYC is dedicated to improving the quality of early childhood programs and can be relied on to provide useful services and information to parents as well as teachers of young children.

1509 16th Street, N.W.

Washington, D.C. 20036-1426

Tel. (800) 424 2460; in D.C., (202) 232-8777

National Academy of Early Childhood Programs

Provides listings of accredited child-care centers and preschools.

1834 Connecticut Avenue, N.W.

Washington, D.C. 20009

Tel. (202) 328-2601

About the Author

For twenty-five years, Doris Herman has been a beloved teacher at Gan HaYeled ("Garden of Children") Preschool in Washington, D.C. After studying psychology at the University of Maryland, she trained in early childhood education at Montgomery College, Maryland, and has taught workshops on the subject to preschool teachers throughout the D.C. metropolitan area. In 1993, the parents of her preschool school created the Doris Herman Foundation to honor excellence in teaching. The foundation presents an annual monetary award to an outstanding preschool teacher. Doris lives in Potomac, Maryland, with her husband, Don. She has three married children and three grandchildren.